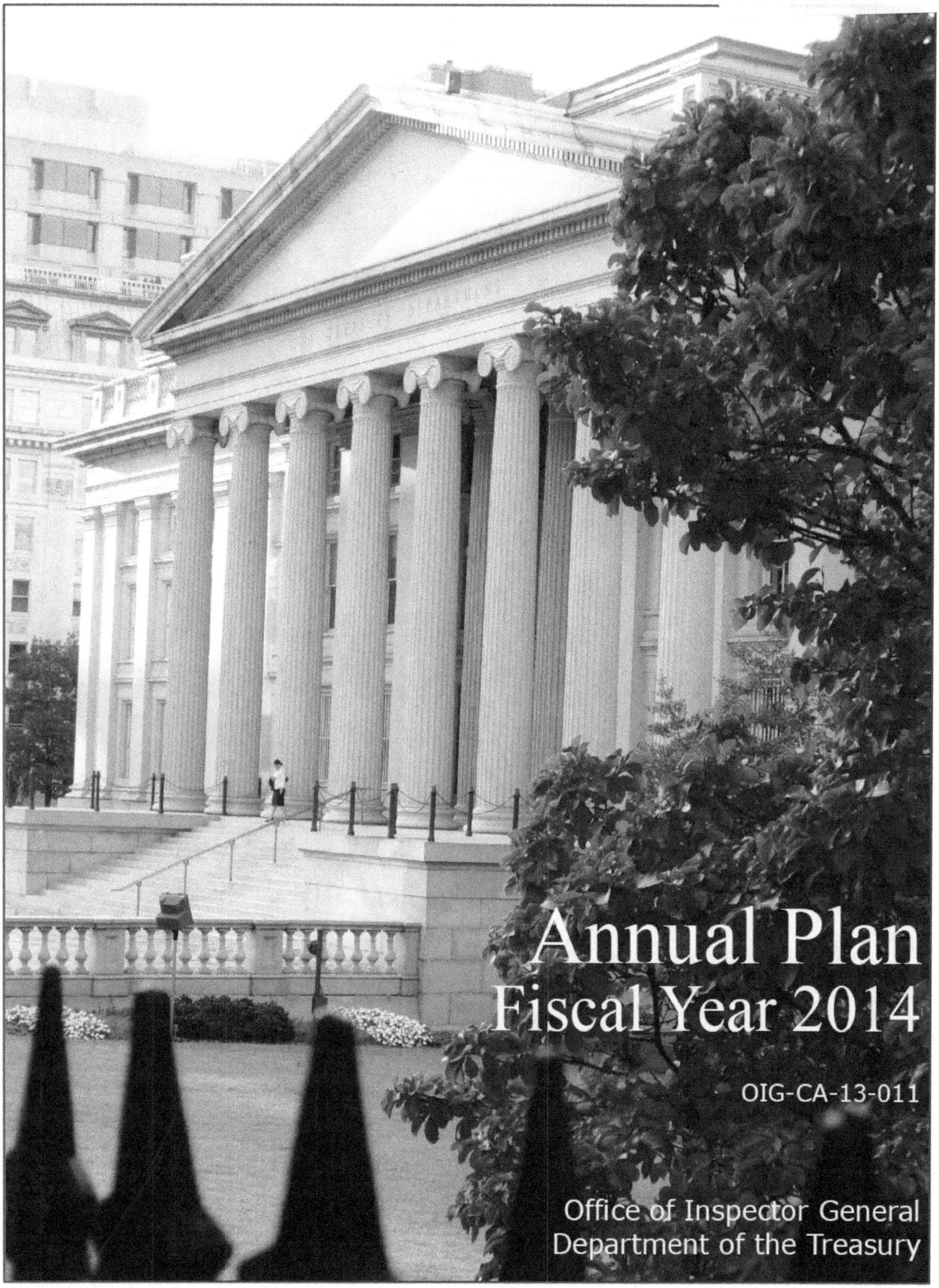

Annual Plan
Fiscal Year 2014

OIG-CA-13-011

Office of Inspector General
Department of the Treasury

Foreword

This annual plan outlines the fiscal year 2014 Department of the Treasury (Treasury) Office of Inspector General (OIG) audit and investigative priorities. The anticipated work focuses on Treasury's major initiatives and challenges, and takes into consideration OIG's *Strategic Plan* for *Fiscal Years 2011-2015*.

We have prioritized our resources to provide oversight of the most significant and highest risk Treasury programs and operations under our jurisdiction. For fiscal year 2014, our highest priorities are oversight efforts related to (1) the Dodd-Frank Wall Street Reform and Consumer Protection Act; (2) the Small Business Jobs Act of 2010; (3) the Bank Secrecy Act and USA PATRIOT Act of 2001; (4) the Resources and Ecosystems Sustainability, Tourist Opportunities, and Revived Economies of the Gulf Coast States Act of 2012 (RESTORE Act); and (5) the "Do Not Pay" Initiative.

Other areas of emphasis for fiscal year 2014 include mandated audits as required by the Government Management Reform Act, the Federal Information Security Management Act, the Federal Deposit Insurance Act, and the Improper Payments acts, among others. This plan also addresses various Congressional directives and areas of interest, including the Financial Crimes Enforcement Network's Bank Secrecy Act information technology modernization program, the Department's consolidation and redesignation of the Financial Management Service and the Bureau of the Public Debt as the Bureau of the Fiscal Service, as well as recent concerns with expenditures for travel, conferences, and awards.

The projects described in this plan address those areas of known and emerging risks and vulnerabilities, based on our assessment. As before, we encourage Department and bureau management to use this plan to identify areas for self-assessment and to take corrective measures when vulnerabilities and control weaknesses are identified.

September 2013

Contents

Overview

Mission Statement

The Department of the Treasury (Treasury) Office of Inspector General (OIG) conducts independent and objective audits and investigations to promote integrity, efficiency, and effectiveness in Treasury's programs and operations.

Background

In 1989, the Secretary of the Treasury established OIG in accordance with the 1988 amendments to the Inspector General Act. As set forth in the act, we

- conduct and supervise audits and investigations of Treasury programs and operations except for the Internal Revenue Service (IRS), which in under the jurisdictional oversight of the Treasury Inspector General for Tax Administration (TIGTA), and the Troubled Asset Relief Program (TARP) which is under the jurisdiction oversight of the Special Inspector General

- provide leadership and coordination of policies that (1) promote economy, efficiency, and effectiveness in Treasury programs and operations and (2) prevent and detect fraud and abuse in Treasury programs and operations

- keep the Secretary of the Treasury and Congress fully and currently informed about problems and deficiencies in Treasury programs and operations

Organizational Structure and Fiscal Resources

OIG is headed by an Inspector General who is appointed by the President with the advice and consent of the Senate. As shown below, OIG's organization is comprised of five offices; all report to the Inspector General and are headquartered in Washington, D.C. OIG also has an audit field office in Boston, Massachusetts.

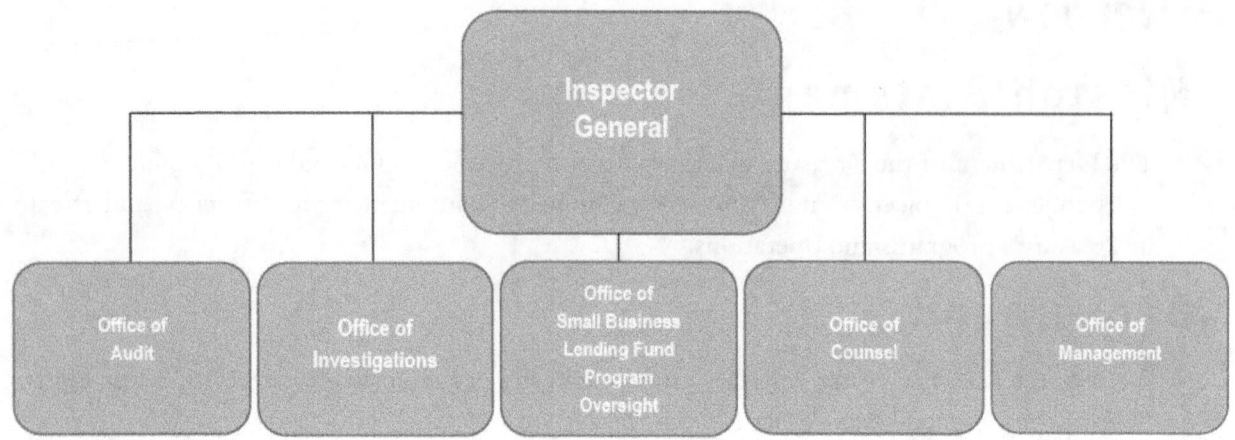

For fiscal year 2014, the President's budget request for direct appropriations for OIG is $31.4 million. The Office of Small Business Lending Fund Program Oversight is funded on a reimbursable basis by the Small Business Lending Fund (SBLF) and the State Small Business Credit Initiative (SSBCI) program offices. Estimated reimbursable funding for fiscal year 2014 is $2.2 million for SBLF oversight and $2.2 million for SSBCI oversight.

Performance Measures

OIG established performance measures for fiscal year 2014 for the Offices of Audit, Investigations, and SBLF Program Oversight.

Office of Audit Performance Measures

- Complete 70 audit products
- Complete 100 percent of mandated audits by the required date
- Identify monetary benefits where appropriate

Office of Investigations Performance Measure

- Ensure 80 percent of investigative work product is referred for civil or criminal prosecution or administratively to a Treasury bureau for appropriate action

Office of SBLF Program Oversight Performance Measures

- Review 20 banks that have received SBLF funds
- Review 10 states allocated SSBCI funds
- Complete 100 percent of mandated SBLF audits by the required date

Fiscal Year 2014 Priorities

Audit Priorities

OIG established three audit priorities for fiscal year 2014.

Priority 1   Audit Products Mandated by Law

OIG allocates significant resources to meet mandated audit requirements, which include (1) audited financial statements and financial-related review work, (2) information security, (3) the Dodd-Frank Wall Street Reform and Consumer Protection Act (Dodd-Frank), (4) Treasury programs authorized by the Small Business Jobs Act, and (5) bank failures pursuant to requirements in the Federal Deposit Insurance Act. We also perform work in response to Congressional directives.

Priority 2   Work Requested by Treasury Management, Congress, or Other External Source

OIG typically receives two to three requests a year from Treasury management or Congress to perform specific work. The requested work is often already in our plan and requires only that we adjust the work schedule or scope. If the requested work is in a new area, we assess whether the work should be performed.

Priority 3   Self-Directed Work in Treasury's Highest-Risk Areas

With the resources available after we have completed mandated audits and requested work, we conduct audits to assess Treasury's progress in addressing significant known and emerging risks and vulnerabilities. For fiscal year 2014, our self-directed work focuses on Treasury's responsibilities as they relate to the implementation of Dodd-Frank; anti-money laundering/terrorist financing programs; Treasury's administration of programs authorized by the Resources and Ecosystems Sustainability, Tourist Opportunities, and Revived Economies of the Gulf Coast States Act of 2012 (RESTORE Act); and Treasury's responsibilities under the Do Not Pay Initiative.

Our planned OIG staff resource utilization by these three priorities for fiscal year 2014 is shown in appendix A.

Treasury OIG Strategic Plan

OIG aligned its *Strategic Plan* for *Fiscal Years 2011-2015* with Treasury's mission to maintain a strong economy and create economic and job opportunities by promoting conditions that enable economic growth and stability at home and abroad, strengthen national security by combating threats and protecting the integrity of the financial system, and manage the U.S. Government's finances and resources. The Treasury OIG mission is to promote the integrity, efficiency, and effectiveness of Treasury programs and operations under its jurisdictional oversight, which is accomplished through four strategic goals:

- Promote the integrity and effectiveness of Treasury programs and operations through audits and investigations

- Proactively support and strengthen the Department's ability to identify and manage challenges, both today and in the future

- Fully and currently inform stakeholders of Treasury OIG findings, recommendations, investigative results, and priorities related to Treasury programs and operations

- Enhance, support, and sustain a workforce and strengthen internal operations to achieve the Treasury OIG mission, vision, and strategic goals

Relationship Between Treasury's Strategic Goals and Treasury OIG's Annual Plan Issue Areas

To accomplish its mission, Treasury identified five strategic goals for fiscal years 2012 to 2015. To support Treasury's strategic goals, OIG will focus its work on nine issue areas.

The following table shows the relationship between four Treasury strategic goals and OIG's nine issue areas. The fifth Treasury strategic goal—pursue comprehensive tax and fiscal reform— principally impacts TIGTA, and is not addressed in this plan.

Treasury Strategic Goal	OIG Issue Area(s)
Repair and reform the financial system and support the recovery of the housing market	• Safety, soundness, and accessibility of financial services
Enhance U.S. competitiveness and promote international financial stability and balanced global growth	• Bill and coin manufacturing, marketing, and distribution operations • Domestic and international assistance programs • SBLF and SSBCI operations • Gulf Coast Restoration Trust Fund oversight
Protect our national security through targeted financial actions	• Terrorist financing, money laundering, and foreign assets control
Manage the government's finances in a fiscally responsible manner	• Treasury general management and infrastructure support • Government-wide financial services and debt management • Revenue collection and industry regulation

Office of Audit Initiatives

The Office of Audit plans to start 88 projects in fiscal year 2014 and complete 44 projects started in prior years. Our ability to initiate new self-directed audits and complete those in progress will be affected by mandated work. We have identified 126 high-priority projects that must be deferred beyond fiscal year 2014. Our in-progress and planned work and projects for future consideration are described in the Planned Projects by OIG Issue Area section of this document.

Investigative Priorities

OIG established four investigative priorities for fiscal year 2014.

Priority 1   Criminal and Serious Employee Misconduct

Our highest priority is investigating complaints involving alleged criminal and other serious misconduct by Treasury employees. OIG investigates allegations of the general crimes enumerated in Title 18 of the U.S. Code, other federal crimes, alleged violations of the Ethics in Government Act, and allegations of serious misconduct prohibited by the Standards of Ethical Conduct for Employees of the Executive Branch. Several Treasury bureaus and offices have additional rules and regulations relating to ethical standards for their own employees and OIG also investigates complaints of alleged violations of these rules and regulations.

Priority 2   Fraud Involving Contracts, Grants, Guarantees, and Funds

We conduct investigations into allegations of fraud and other crimes involving Treasury contracts, grants, loan guarantees, and federal funds. Such allegations often involve contractors, entities, and individuals who are providing or seeking to provide goods or services to the Department. We receive complaints alleging criminal or other misconduct from employees, contractors, members of the public, and the Congress.

Priority 3   Financial Programs and Operations Crime

We conduct and supervise investigations relating to Treasury financial programs and operations. These programs and operations involve issuing licenses, providing benefits, and exercising oversight of U.S. financial institutions.

Priority 4   Threats Against Treasury Employees and Facilities

Our investigative efforts into threats against Treasury employees and facilities are critical in ensuring safety for the Department. These matters require prompt attention and coordination with federal, state, and local authorities in order to protect those involved.

Office of SBLF Program Oversight Initiatives

The Office of SBLF Program Oversight plans to start 4 SBLF audits and 13 SSBCI state reviews in fiscal year 2014. Our in-progress and planned work and projects for future consideration are described in the Planned Projects by OIG Issue Area section of this document.

Counsel Initiatives

The Office of Counsel supports OIG investigative, oversight, and audit activities by responding to requests for legal advice and reviewing and processing requests for the issuance of Inspector General subpoenas. In the area of disclosure, the office will provide timely responses to Freedom of Information Act (FOIA) and Privacy Act requests. It will carry out its litigation responsibilities in Merit Systems Protection Board and Equal Employment Opportunity Commission cases, as necessary. Based on experience, the Office of Counsel expects to process 50 initial FOIA/Privacy Act requests and 3 appeals from those initial responses. In the area of electronic FOIA, the office expects to review approximately 80 audit, evaluation, and oversight reports for posting on OIG's website. It will also

- provide ethics and standards of conduct training for all employees, and timely review all required confidential and public financial disclosure reports;

- review and update, as needed, Privacy Impact Assessments for all OIG operations and provide procedural review and training services as the OIG senior agency official for privacy;

- respond to *Giglio*[1] requests, coordinate responses to document requests from Congress, and respond to discovery requests arising from litigation involving the Department and its bureaus;

- provide training on the Inspector General Act and other subjects in connection with new employee orientation and in-service training;

- review, as statutorily mandated, legislative and regulatory proposals and, where appropriate, coordinate comments; and

- review all allegations of misuse of the Treasury seal, name, and identification; and prepare cease and desist orders and penalty assessments, as needed, to carry out OIG's authority to enforce Title 31 of the U.S. Code, Section 333, Prohibition of misuse of Department of the Treasury names, symbols, etc.

Management Initiatives

The Office of Management provides OIG offices with a full range of administrative support, including budget and finance, facilities management, procurement, human resources, security, records management, asset management, and information technology (IT) services. The office is augmented by a working agreement with the Bureau of the Fiscal Service's (BFS) Administrative Resource Center for travel, budget execution, and accounting services.

During fiscal year 2014, the Office of Management will focus on providing timely, quality, and forward-thinking service to OIG customers. In addition, the office will continue to identify operational efficiencies to improve management support while identifying opportunities to reduce cost. In particular, it will look to reduce costs for travel, conferences, and fleet management in accordance with the Office of Management and Budget's (OMB) guidance, while ensuring that critical oversight and investigative activities continue.

The office's administrative services component will update and strengthen policies and procedures, manage the purchase card program, all purchase requests over the $3,000 threshold, and the travel program. It will also promote the use of public transportation and administer the public transit

---

[1] *Giglio* is information that refers to material that may call into question the character or testimony of a prosecution witness in a criminal trial.

program, oversee security and safety initiatives, and implement OIG's long-range plan for space needs. During 2014, the administrative services component will be working closely with the Department and U.S. General Services Administration to identify space needs in anticipation of a possible relocation of OIG components from two locations to one location in 2015. A major focus will be institutionalizing policies and procedures for in-house procurement services.

During fiscal year 2014, OIG Security will continue to manage the development of a Personal Identify Verification (PIV) Data Synchronization business process map showing linkages to HRConnect and USAccess for employee sponsorship and PIV card issuance. Security services include initiating and adjudicating required background investigations, granting security clearances for access to classified information, maintaining electronic database records, providing verification of security clearances, and processing requests for access to Sensitive Compartmented Information. In addition, Office of Management (OM) will take additional steps in implementing, testing and training employees regarding continuity of operations planning to include emergency evacuation and shelter-in-place procedures.

The Office of Management's budget and finance component will work with the Administrative Resource Center to increase the timeliness of financial information and accuracy of budget projections, while adapting to the uncertainties of the federal budgeting process. The office will continue to provide for the efficient and effective reconciliation of financial transactions. It will also provide monitoring and oversight of billing and invoice approvals to ensure full compliance with the Prompt Pay Act, and OMB's Do Not Pay Initiative, prepare and execute interagency agreements for services provided or rendered, respond to budget data calls, and act as liaison to the Administrative Resource Center for any system changes that impact OIG budgeting or accounting.

Treasury's Management and Performance Challenges

In accordance with the Reports Consolidation Act of 2000, the Treasury Inspector General annually provides the Secretary of the Treasury with his perspective on the most serious management and performance challenges facing the Department. In a memorandum to Secretary Geithner dated October 25, 2012, Inspector General Thorson reported one new challenge—Gulf Coast Restoration Trust Fund Administration—and three challenges from the prior year. One previously reported challenge was removed. The following is a synopsis of the matters included in that memorandum. The Inspector General's annual Management and Performance Challenges Memoranda are available on the OIG's website.

Transformation of Financial Regulation (Repeat Challenge)

This challenge focuses on the responsibilities of Treasury and the Secretary under Dodd-Frank.

Management of Treasury's Authorities Intended to Support and Improve the Economy (Repeat Challenge)

This challenge focuses on the administration of broad authorities given to Treasury by the Congress to address the financial crisis under the Housing and Economic Recovery Act of 2008, the Emergency Economic Stabilization Act of 2008, the American Recovery and Reinvestment Act of 2009, and the Small Business Jobs Act of 2010.

Anti-Money Laundering and Terrorist Financing/Bank Secrecy Act Enforcement (Repeat Challenge)

This challenge focuses on the difficulties Treasury faces to ensure criminals and terrorists do not use our financial networks to sustain their operations and/or launch attacks against the U.S.

Gulf Coast Restoration Trust Fund Administration

This challenge focuses on Treasury's administration of a new activity, the Gulf Coast Restoration Trust Fund, established by the Resources and Ecosystems Sustainability, Tourist Opportunities, and Revived Economies of the Gulf Coast States Act of 2012 (RESTORE Act) in response to the April 2010 Deepwater Horizon oil spill.

Our memorandum also highlighted three areas of concern—cyber threats, challenges with currency and coin production, and lapses by the Department in maintaining a complete and concurrent record of key activities and decisions. Additionally, we noted challenges faced by the Department as it undertakes the consolidation and restructuring of the Bureau of the Public Debt (BPD) and Financial Management Service (FMS) into the Bureau of the Fiscal Service (BFS).

In October 2013, the Inspector General will update the above management and performance challenges in a memorandum to the Secretary.

Planned Projects by OIG Issue Area

Treasury General Management and Infrastructure Support: Financial Management

Issue Area Discussion

Mandates

Financial audits are required for the Department and certain component entities pursuant to various statutes and other reporting requirements. The annual audit of Treasury's consolidated financial statements is performed pursuant to the Government Management Reform Act. OMB designated IRS as a Treasury component entity required to issue stand-alone audited financial statements under the act. Other Treasury component entities required to have stand-alone audited financial statements are the Bureau of Engraving and Printing (BEP), the Exchange Stabilization Fund, the Federal Financing Bank, the U.S. Mint (Mint), the Treasury Forfeiture Fund, the Office of D.C. Pensions, the Community Development Financial Institutions (CDFI) Fund, the Office of the Comptroller of the Currency (OCC), and the Office of Financial Stability. The Alcohol and Tobacco Tax and Trade Bureau (TTB) financial statements are audited as a management initiative. In addition, certain accounts and activities of BFS that are material to the Department's financial statements are also audited.

Independent public accounting firms, under contract with the OIG, audit the Department's consolidated financial statements and the financial statements of component entities, with some exceptions. The Government Accountability Office (GAO) audits the IRS's and the Office of Financial Stability's financial statements, and BFS' Schedule of Federal Debt. Additionally, OIG staff audit the Mint's Schedule of Custodial Deep Storage Gold and Silver Reserves and Treasury's Schedule of United States Gold Reserves Held by Federal Reserve Banks.

Program Responsibilities

Treasury also has responsibility for certain programs that will be reviewed as part of the audit of the fiscal year 2014 Department-wide financial statements including programs established by (1) the Housing and Economic Recovery Act of 2008 (HERA), (2) the Emergency Economic Stabilization Act of 2008, (3) the American Recovery and Reinvestment Act of 2009 (Recovery Act), (4) the Small Business Jobs Act of 2010, and (5) the Terrorism Risk Insurance Extension Act of 2005 as reauthorized by the Terrorism Risk Insurance Reauthorization Act of 2007.

The purpose of the terrorism risk insurance program enacted under the terrorism risk insurance acts is to stabilize market disruptions that result from acts of terrorism. The program, which expires December 31, 2014, and has a cap on annual liability for insured losses of $100 billion, is in place to pay 85 percent of the insured losses arising from acts of terrorism above insurers' deductibles. Other programs established by the acts listed above are discussed in the Domestic and International Assistance Programs and SBLF and SSBCI Operations issue areas of this plan.

Working Capital Fund

The Department maintains the Working Capital Fund to centrally provide common administrative services across the Department and thereby achieve economies of scale and eliminate duplication of effort. These services are provided on a reimbursable basis to Treasury components at rates that recover the fund's operating expenses. For fiscal year 2012, Working Capital Fund expenses were approximately $146 million.

Improper Payments

The Improper Payments Elimination and Recovery Act of 2010 (IPERA) requires each agency to periodically review all programs and activities susceptible to significant improper payments. If a determination is made that a program is susceptible to significant improper payments, the agency must (1) estimate the amount of the improper payments, (2) report on actions that the agency is taking to reduce improper payments, (3) report on actions the agency is taking to recover improper payments, and (4) include this information in the accompanying materials to the annual financial statements. The act also requires agencies to conduct recovery audits of each program and activity that expends more than $1 million annually, if not prohibited by law and if it would be cost effective. The inspector general of each agency is required to annually determine if the agency is in compliance with the act.

The Improper Payments Elimination and Recovery Improvement Act of 2012 (IPERIA) builds on IPERA. Among other things, IPERIA requires OMB to (1) annually identify a list of high priority federal programs with the highest dollar value, rate, or higher risk of improper payment for greater levels of oversight and review and (2) coordinate with agencies responsible for administering these high priority federal programs to establish annual targets and semi-annual or quarterly actions for reducing improper payments associated with each program. Each agency with a high priority federal program is required to annually submit to its Inspector General, and make available to the public, a report that describes actions the agency has taken or plans to take to recover improper payments and actions it intends to take to prevent future improper payments.

Managerial Cost Accounting

Managerial cost accounting involves the accumulation and analysis of financial and nonfinancial data, resulting in the allocation of costs to organizational pursuits such as performance goals, programs, activities, and outputs, and should be a fundamental part of a financial performance management system. Both our office and GAO have reported the need for Treasury to more effectively implement managerial cost accounting. The Department developed a high-level managerial cost accounting implementation plan and revised its managerial cost accounting policy to improve managerial cost accounting practices throughout Treasury, promote consistency wherever possible, and address OIG and GAO concerns.

Known Weaknesses

The Department received an unqualified audit opinion on its fiscal year 2012 consolidated financial statements. The independent public accounting firm's audit report disclosed the following internal control deficiencies:

- Material weakness in internal control over financial reporting at the IRS (repeat condition)
- Significant deficiency in internal control in information systems controls at BFS (repeat condition)

The auditor also reported that the Department's financial management systems did not substantially comply with the requirements of the Federal Financial Management Improvement Act related to federal financial management system requirements and applicable federal accounting standards.

In-Progress and Planned Fiscal Year 2014 Projects

Audits of Treasury Financial Statements and of Financial Statements or Schedules for Component Entities and Activities (Ongoing)

During fiscal year 2014, we will complete audit work for the fiscal year 2013 financial statements and schedules and begin audit work for the fiscal year 2014 financial statements and schedules. These audits will determine if the financial statements and schedules are fairly presented in all material respects and will report on internal control, compliance with laws and regulations, and compliance with the Federal Financial Management Improvement Act.

Treasury's Compliance With the Improper Payments Elimination and Recovery Act of 2010 (Ongoing)

We will determine Treasury's compliance with this act. We plan to work with TIGTA to provide an overall assessment of Treasury's compliance.

Improper Payments Elimination and Recovery Improvement Act of 2012 Review (Ongoing)

For each Treasury non-IRS high priority federal program, we will review (1) the assessment of the level of risk, (2) the quality of Treasury's improper payment estimates and methodology used to calculate the estimates, and (3) Treasury's oversight of financial controls to identify and prevent improper payments. In addition, as applicable, we will submit to Congress recommendations for modifying any Treasury plans relating to each program including improvements for improper payments determination and the estimation methodology.

Controls Over the Review of Unliquidated Obligations

In light of the sequestration and necessary budget cuts, effective management and review of appropriated budgetary resources is imperative. Unliquidated obligations are obligations of budgetary resources that have been incurred but not paid for, such as an account payable for an item ordered or received but not yet paid for. At September 30, 2012, Treasury's total unpaid obligations were $142 billion. Reviews of unliquidated obligations are necessary to properly report obligation balances, certify the validity of obligated balances, and make funds available for expenditure that otherwise would not be used.

We plan to assess Treasury and non-IRS component entity management controls and procedures over the review of unliquidated obligations.

Cash Discounts

A cash discount is a reduction to the amount of an invoice that a seller offers a buyer in exchange for paying an invoice before its scheduled payment due date. Considering the high volume of bills paid by Treasury, significant savings can be achieved by taking advantage of cash discounts.

The Treasury Financial Manual (TFM) provides a methodology to follow to determine if a cash discount should be taken. The TFM requires that agency payment systems incorporate procedures that take advantage of cash discounts as a matter of routine.

We plan to assess the TFM's cash discounts policy and determine if Treasury and its components are adhering to it to take full advantage of cash discount opportunities.

Projects under Consideration for Future Fiscal Years

Working Capital Fund

We plan to determine if the Department established adequate controls over the Working Capital Fund. As part of the overall audit, we plan to determine if: (1) fund activities and programs are appropriate for inclusion in the fund; (2) reconciliations between actual costs incurred by the fund and costs billed to participating Treasury bureaus exist, are timely prepared, and consistent; (3) costs charged by the fund are appropriate; (4) costs charged by the fund to specific bureaus are supported by appropriate documentation; and (5) assumptions, data, processes, and models used by the fund to estimate its annual costs are reasonable. We will coordinate our work as necessary with TIGTA.

Survey of XBRL

The eXtensible Business Reporting Language (XBRL) is a standards-based way to communicate and exchange business information between business systems. These communications capture reporting concepts as well as the relationships and other meanings commonly required in business reporting. It can offer cost savings, greater efficiency and improved accuracy and reliability to those involved in supplying or using financial data.

We plan to assess whether XBRL can offer Treasury improved business capabilities for managing its programs and operations.

Managerial Cost Accounting

We plan to assess whether Treasury implemented managerial cost accounting comprehensively and effectively.

Office of D.C. Pensions' Quality Assurance Program Over Annuitant Benefit Payments

The Office of D.C. Pensions implements the Secretary's responsibilities under the Balanced Budget Act of 1997 to make timely and accurate federal benefit payments associated with the D.C. Retirement Programs for police officers, firefighters, teachers, and judges. These benefit payments totaled $544 million in 2012. During past financial statement audits, the auditor identified errors in annuitant payment amounts.

We plan to determine if the Office of D.C. Pensions' quality assurance program over annuitant payments is designed and operating effectively to detect and correct mistakes in annuitant benefit payment processing.

Treasury General Management and Infrastructure Support: Information Security

Issue Area Discussion

External threats to Treasury's infrastructure and information include terrorists, criminals, and computer hackers. Malicious cyber threats have increased at an unprecedented rate with so many hacking tools and malware becoming more readily available and relatively easy to use. In addition, insider threats remain a serious concern. Examples of these acts include, but are not limited to, modifying or stealing confidential or sensitive information; theft of trade secrets or customer information for business or personal advantage; and sabotage of data, systems, or networks. As insiders have significant knowledge of Treasury's policies, procedures, technology, and vulnerabilities in networks or systems, they can bypass physical and technical security measures designed to prevent external threats. Because of the nature of Treasury's missions, ensuring the effectiveness of information security controls is paramount to prevent attacks and defend against malicious outsiders and insiders from doing the following:

- disrupting key Treasury functions (e.g., collection of revenues, issuing payments, managing the government's cash and debt, producing coins and currency, and preventing financial crimes)
- compromising classified or sensitive Treasury information
- obtaining or disclosing private citizen information
- destroying or altering information needed to accomplish Treasury's missions
- stealing valuable equipment or technology
- inappropriately using Treasury resources

In addition, the dynamics of cyberspace and technical innovations (e.g., e-commerce, social networking, and mobile devices) that provide greater convenience and accessibility to users also increases vulnerabilities to Treasury's information and resources. Because IT plays a crucial role in accomplishing all of Treasury's strategic objectives and activities, it is vital for Treasury to have an information security program that ensures the integrity of Treasury's information systems and the reliability and confidentiality of its data.

Mandates

The Federal Information Security Management Act (FISMA) requires OIG to issue an annual independent evaluation of the effectiveness of Treasury's information security program and practices. TIGTA conducts the evaluation of IRS's information security program and practices. An independent public accountant, under contract with OIG, conducts the evaluation of Treasury's remaining unclassified security systems, incorporating TIGTA's evaluation into Treasury's overall results. We may from year-to-year exercise a contract option to conduct the unclassified security systems evaluation as an audit. In addition, we may from year-to-year exercise a contract option to perform the FISMA evaluation covering Treasury's collateral national security systems. OIG staff conducts the FISMA audit of Treasury's intelligence national security systems.

Based on the results of the fiscal year 2012 FISMA audit, we reported that Treasury's information security program for unclassified systems was in place and generally consistent with FISMA. However, the program for Treasury's non-IRS unclassified systems was not fully effective in the areas of logical account management, security incident reporting, system security plan, audit log review, plans of action and milestones, vulnerability scanning and remediation, contingency planning and testing, backup controls, system configuration settings, system baselines, and multifactor authentication.

Program Responsibilities

Under OMB's 25-Point Implementation Plan to Reform Federal IT Management, dated December 9, 2010, agencies were to (1) turn around or terminate at least one-third of underperforming projects in IT portfolio within 18 months, (2) shift to a Cloud First policy, and (3) reduce the number of federal data centers by at least 800 by 2015. Under OMB's Cloud First policy, federal agencies must identify three "must-move" services within 3 months and move one of those services to the cloud within 12 months and the remaining two within 18 months. Treasury was the first cabinet-level agency to move its public facing website, Treasury.gov, into the cloud for the stated purpose of improving the way citizens access Treasury data and information. Treasury.gov is the largest of multiple systems which Treasury hosts on public cloud, including FinancialStability.gov, MakingHomeAffordable.gov, SIGTARP.gov, and MyMoney.gov. Treasury had also identified other services, which have migrated to cloud solutions, such as Document Management and FOIA Case Management, Bureau of the Consumer Financial Protection's Data Center Services, and BEP's Business Process Management. In addition, BFS contracted with Oracle to use Oracle on-Demand cloud services as hosting and infrastructure support for systems used to provide administrative services to other federal entities. With current trends in consolidation and hosting new systems on the cloud, assuring compliance of cloud-based systems with appropriate security requirements will be essential.

In February 2010, OMB launched the Federal Data Center Consolidation Initiative to assist agencies in identifying their existing data center assets and to formulate consolidation plans that include a technical roadmap and consolidation targets. The initiative addresses the growth of data centers and assists agencies in leveraging best practices from the public and private sector to:

- promote the use of green IT by reducing the overall energy and real estate footprint of government data centers;
- reduce the cost of data center hardware, software, and operations;
- increase the overall IT security posture of the government; and
- shift IT investments to more efficient computing platforms and technologies.

In its September 2011 Data Center Consolidation Plan, Treasury reported it has 55 data center facilities and server rooms housed, with an additional 14 facilities in commercial banks or Federal

Reserve Banks (FRBs). Treasury has targeted to reduce its data centers to 40 by 2015. Treasury's data center consolidation will require a restructuring of Treasury's IT infrastructure in a relatively short timeframe to meet OMB reduction targets. The Treasury Data Center Consolidation Plan incorporated a move towards virtualization. Treasury has targeted to increase server virtualization to 50 percent by 2015. This calculation uses the number of virtual hosts over total servers, where total servers equals physical servers plus virtual hosts. Virtualization is part of an overall trend in enterprise IT that allows an IT environment to manage itself, where users pay for only the IT they use. The goal of virtualization is to centralize administrative tasks, improve scalability, and improve overall hardware resource utilization. With virtualization, several operating systems can be run in parallel on a single central processing unit. This parallelism can reduce overhead costs and is thus an attractive method for federal agencies to realize cost savings. At the same time, full virtualization has security implications. In addition to adding layers of technology,which can increase the security burden, combining many systems onto a single physical computer can cause a larger impact if a security compromise occurs. In some cases, virtualized environments are quite dynamic, which makes creating and maintaining the necessary security boundaries more complex.

America's critical cyber infrastructure consists of government and private sector systems and assets that are vital to public confidence and the nation's safety, prosperity, and well-being. These systems are increasingly at risk of falling victim to a cyberattack that could cripple the nation's infrastructure and economy. There have been a number of high profile cyberattacks against the financial sector. The President highlighted this threat in the 2013 State of the Union Address, and recent Congressional testimony has illustrated the threats to America's critical cyber infrastructure. In response to this threat, the President signed Presidential Policy Directive 21 to promote a cybersecurity partnership between the government and the private companies that oversee America's critical infrastructure. The executive order (E.O.) requires Treasury to collaborate with the Department of Homeland Security and financial sector organizations to identify and protect critical cyber infrastructure. Effective public-private coordination will be required to address the growing threat of cyberattacks against America's critical infrastructure. Treasury systems are interconnected and critical to the core functions of the government and the Nation's financial infrastructure. Information security remains a constant area of concern and potential vulnerability for Treasury's network and systems. Therefore, it is critical that Treasury be prepared to provide leadership to defend against cyber threats to financial institutions' critical infrastructure.

In fiscal year 2011, OMB issued Memorandum M-11-33, *FY 2011 Reporting Instructions for the Federal Information Security Management Act and Agency Privacy Management*, and emphasized monitoring the security state of information systems on an ongoing basis with a frequency sufficient to make ongoing, risk-based decisions. National Institute of Technology Special Publication 800-137, *Information Security Continuous Monitoring for Federal Information Systems and Organization*, dated September 2011, defines continuous monitoring as maintaining ongoing awareness of information security, vulnerabilities, and threats to support organizational risk management decisions. The federal cybersecurity Cross Agency Priority Goal for executive branch departments and agencies was to achieve 95 percent implementation of the Administration's priority cybersecurity capabilities by the end of fiscal year 2014. Among these capabilities is continuous monitoring, which must be effective to provide ongoing, real-time risk management and operational security for IT systems and to ensure security controls being used on IT systems are effective and appropriate for the level of risk tolerance.

In-Progress and Planned Fiscal Year 2014 Projects

FISMA Independent Evaluation—Unclassified Systems (Ongoing)

We will determine if Treasury's information security program and practices, as they relate to Treasury's unclassified security systems, are consistent with FISMA. We will also assess progress made in resolving previously reported FISMA weaknesses. During fiscal year 2014, we will complete audit work for fiscal year 2013 and begin work for fiscal year 2014.

FISMA Independent Evaluation—Collateral National Security Systems (Ongoing)

We will determine if Treasury's information security program and practices, as they relate to Treasury's collateral national security systems, are consistent with FISMA. We will also assess progress made in resolving previously reported FISMA weaknesses. During fiscal year 2014, we will complete audit work for fiscal year 2013 and begin audit work for fiscal year 2014.

FISMA Independent Audit for Fiscal Year 2014—Intelligence National Security Systems (Ongoing)

We will determine if Treasury's information security program and practices, as they relate to Treasury's intelligence national security systems, are consistent with FISMA. We will also assess progress made in resolving previously reported FISMA weaknesses.

Network and System Security Assessments

We plan to determine if effective security measures exist to detect and prevent unauthorized access to Treasury bureaus' networks and systems. To accomplish this objective, we plan to identify and exploit existing vulnerabilities in IT infrastructure to determine if network-connected systems are (1) secure from unauthorized intrusion and misuse, (2) vulnerable to malicious security attacks, or (3) accessible through unauthorized or misconfigured paths (e.g., backdoors into the network from the internet or adjacent networks). In this regard, we plan to perform a coordinated network security test by conducting automated and manual vulnerability assessments and exploitation. For fiscal year 2014, we plan to conduct audits at the Financial Crimes Enforcement Network (FinCEN), Mint, and OIG.

Security Protection of Treasury Data in Cloud Computing Environment (In-Progress)

We plan to determine if Treasury ensured effective security protection for its data in the cloud computing environment. During fiscal year 2014, we will complete our audit work at BFS and begin an audit at the Departmental Offices.

Security Controls Over Virtual Servers Located in BFS' Consolidated Data Centers (In-Progress)

We plan to determine if proper controls are in place for securing servers and employing virtualization technology that are located in BFS' consolidated data centers.

Security Controls Over BEP's Industrial Control Systems

Industrial control systems in a manufacturing environment encompass several types of control systems including supervisory control and data acquisition systems, distributed control systems, and other control system configurations.

We plan to determine if BEP has provided effective security controls over its industrial control systems.

Security Assessment of Treasury's Collateral National Security Systems

We plan to determine if sufficient protections exist to prevent intrusions into Treasury's national security systems. To accomplish this objective, we will assess vulnerabilities that allow intruders or insiders to bypass security controls that protect system confidentiality, integrity, and availability.

Continuous Monitoring Program

We plan to determine if Treasury has an effective continuous monitoring program to maintain ongoing awareness and assessment of information security risks and rapidly respond to support organizational risk management decisions.

Mobile Device Security

We plan to determine if Treasury has provided proper safeguards over mobile devices.

Disaster Recovery Exercises

We plan to determine if Treasury and its components can recover operations in the event of a disaster. We will observe scheduled disaster recovery exercises on a selective basis. During fiscal year 2014, we plan to observe one exercise.

Projects Under Consideration for Future Fiscal Years

Software License Management

We plan to determine if Treasury owns and tracks software licenses installed on its systems.

Wireless Local Area Network Security

We plan to determine if Treasury implemented security management practices and controls over wireless local area networks that meet federal guidelines.

Trusted Internet Connection Compliance

In November 2007, OMB issued Memorandum M-08-05, *Implementation of Trusted Internet Connections*, as an initiative to optimize individual network services into a common solution for the federal government. This common solution facilitates the reduction of external connections, including Internet points of presence, to a target of 50. Each agency was required to develop a comprehensive plan of action and milestones with a target completion date of June 2008.

We plan to determine if Treasury's offices and bureaus have complied with OMB's Trusted Internet Connection initiative. We will also determine if the bureaus have connections to the Internet outside of the approved trusted Internet Connections, and if they do, we will determine how they mitigate vulnerabilities associated with that access.

Financial Cyber Critical Infrastructure Protection

We plan to assess Treasury's coordination efforts with other government and private sector entities to protect the nation's banking and finance critical cyber infrastructure.

Protection of Treasury's Designated Cyber Critical Infrastructure

We plan to determine if Treasury established protection and resilience for its designated cyber critical infrastructure.

Enterprise Patch Management

We plan to determine if Treasury's offices and bureaus have a patch management program to ensure timely and secure installation of software patches.

Treasury's Use of Contractors for IT

We plan to determine the extent Treasury uses contractors in its IT-related programs and whether controls are in place to ensure contractors provide goods and services in accordance with their contracts.

Treasury's Government Security Operations Center Services

We plan to determine if Treasury's Government Security Operations Center is analyzing security related events and data that traverse the Treasury-wide sensitive but unclassified communications network (TNet), as well as approved Internet access points across the Department.

Mission Critical Databases Security

We plan to determine if Treasury has implemented security controls over its mission critical database management systems.

Equipment Sanitation and Disposal

We plan to determine if Treasury's offices and bureaus use media sanitization and disposal techniques consistent with the security categorization of the associated system's confidentiality.

Intrusion Detection and Incident Response

We plan to assess Treasury's intrusion detection and incident response programs, policies, and procedures.

Firewall Security

We plan to determine if Treasury has configured its firewalls to prevent unauthorized access attempts into its network and systems.

Social Media

We plan to determine if Treasury's use of social media complies with policy guidance and applicable laws.

25 Point Implementation

We plan to determine Treasury's progress towards meeting the goals of OMB's 25 Point Execution Plan.

Voice Over Internet Protocol

We plan to determine if the Treasury has implemented security controls over voice over internet protocol phones.

Integrating Information Security into Capital Planning

We plan to determine if Treasury has integrated information security into the capital planning and investment control process in accordance with federal guidelines.

Treasury General Management and Infrastructure Support: General Management

Issue Area Discussion

In addition to financial management and information security, the Treasury General Management and Infrastructure Support issue area encompasses other management activities to ensure that resources are used efficiently and effectively to carry out Treasury programs and operations. Examples of broad management activities that warrant audit coverage are discussed below.

Capital Investments

Sound business practices for the acquisition and maintenance of information systems (including hardware and software) are necessary to support Treasury's mission to effectively manage resources. Absent such practices, Treasury may

- inadvertently develop or acquire duplicate or incompatible systems;
- pay higher prices for commercial off-the-shelf products by not obtaining volume discounts;
- develop systems that do not address Treasury's needs or provide management with information needed to accomplish key missions;
- exceed projected or reasonable costs to develop, acquire, or maintain systems;
- acquire or develop systems that do not secure and protect Treasury's classified, confidential, or sensitive information; or
- implement systems that do not readily integrate with existing systems.

Under the Clinger-Cohen Act of 1996, agencies are required to submit business plans for IT investments to OMB. In 2009, OMB instituted the IT Dashboard website where agencies report details of their IT investments. This site allows users to track the progress of IT projects over time. To identify IT projects at risk for excess costs or schedule delays, the costs and progress are rated against the agency's plan. As of May 2013, Treasury non-IRS bureaus reported 35 major IT investments. Of these projects, the Treasury Chief Information Officer reported 4 IT projects as having medium risk to accomplishing their goals—Central Accounting and Reporting System; Payment Application Modernization; Over the Counter Channel Application; and Treasury Enterprise Identity, Credential and Access Management. The first two projects are also identified as expected to be delayed and exceed projected costs. Projects identified with medium overall risk and high-risk in cost and scheduling require special attention from the highest level of agency management but are not necessarily at risk of failure.

Past audits indicated that Treasury did not always effectively manage its capital investments, although we have reported much improved management was in place over more recent on-going projects. Certain capital investments, such as those for telecommunications, are funded through the

Department's Working Capital Fund. Such projects do not receive the same scrutiny by OMB and Congress as those projects that are directly funded through the typical, direct, appropriations process.

Procurement

Procurements are a major Treasury activity. For example, between October 2012 and April 2013, Treasury non-IRS bureaus issued $2.4 billion in contract actions. Of that amount, $1.9 billion was issued by the Mint for metals. Also, the use of government credit cards for micro purchases (generally goods and services under $3,000) is extensive, and strong control over this activity is essential to prevent abuse as recognized by the passage of the Government Charge Card and Prevention Act of 2012.

In 2011, Treasury transferred a portion the Department's contract activities to IRS. Two (2) years later in 2013, the Department transferred bureau procurement activities, except for manufacturing actions, to either BFS or IRS.

OIG is the Department's focal point for obtaining pre-award, costs incurred, and other contract audits requested by Treasury offices and the bureaus, except for IRS. These audits are typically performed by the Defense Contract Audit Agency and coordinated through our office.

Nonappropriated Activities

Three Treasury bureaus—BEP, the Mint, and OCC—do not receive appropriated funds; instead, they operate with revolving funds. BEP and the Mint charge the Board of Governors of the Federal Reserve System for manufactured goods, while OCC assesses fees to those banks under its supervision for regulatory activities. These three bureaus generally have greater latitude than Treasury's appropriated bureaus in how they finance their operations. Other revolving funds are administered by the Deputy CFO (Working Capital Fund) and BFS' Administrative Resource Center.

Potential Integrity Risks

Potential integrity risks may result from the actions of external parties (contractors, terrorists, drug lords, and hackers) or internal personnel (disgruntled or unethical employees). Internal personnel, for example, can disrupt Treasury functions, violate laws, award contracts for less than best value, receive bribes or kickbacks, steal or reveal sensitive data, and cost the taxpayer money through the theft of materials and machinery, finished products, and mutilated products.

In-Progress and Planned Fiscal Year 2014 Projects

Corrective Action Verifications (On-going)

Treasury and bureau management are responsible for implementing agreed-to audit recommendations made by OIG. Management records its planned corrective actions in response to audit recommendations and the completion of those actions in the Joint Audit Management Enterprise System (JAMES), Treasury's audit recommendation tracking system.

We plan to determine if management has taken corrective action responsive to the intent of selected recommendations from prior OIG audit reports. In selecting recommendations for verification, we also consider recommendations that have been open more than a year to assess progress made toward implementing planned actions. Audit reports for which we plan to conduct corrective aaction verifications during fiscal year 2014 include (1) *Consultation on Solyndra Loan Guarantee Was Rushed,* (OIG-12-048; Apr. 3, 2012), and (2) *Bill Manufacturing: Improved Planning and Production Oversight Over NexGen $100 Note Is Critical,* (OIG-12-038; Jan. 24, 2012).

Contract Audit Oversight Activities (Ongoing)

We plan to oversee and coordinate Defense Contract Audit Agency contract audit services requested by Treasury procurement officers.

Controls Over Purchase and Travel Cards (On-Going)

As required by the Government Charge Card Abuse Prevention Act of 2012, we will assess the Treasury purchase card and travel card programs to identify and analyze risks of illegal, improper, or erroneous purchases, travel charges, or payments in order to develop a plan for using such risk assessments to determine the scope, frequency, and number of periodic audits of purchase card or convenience check transactions and travel charge card transactions. We also plan to prepare joint reports with the Department as applicable under the act on violations or other actions related to Treasury purchase card and convenience check guidance or illegal, improper, or erroneous purchases with purchase cards or convenience checks.

Controls Over Travel, Conferences, and Employee Awards Programs (In-Progress)

We plan to determine if Treasury bureaus have effective policies and procedures in place to ensure compliance with all applicable federal laws, regulations, and executive orders on travel, conferences, and employee awards programs. We are undertaking this work pursuant to Section 631 of the House Report 112-550.

Treasury Office of Security (In Progress)

We plan to determine if (1) controls are implemented to ensure security clearance activities are conducted in a timely and appropriate manner and (2) security-related documents are secured.

Treasury Procurement Activities (In-Progress)

We plan to determine if selected Treasury bureaus and offices follow logical and prudent business practices that comply with laws and regulations and Treasury policies and procedures when procuring goods and services. We have audits in progress at OCC. During fiscal year 2014, we plan to initiate separate audits of the Office of Financial Research and the Mint.

Offices of Minority and Women Inclusion (In Progress)

We plan to determine if the Department and OCC followed the requirements of Dodd-Frank in creating Offices of Minority and Women Inclusion. As of September 2013, we had an audit in progress at Departmental Office. We plan to initiate an audit at OCC in fiscal year 2014.

Treasury Enterprise Identity, Credential and Access Management

In 2012, the Treasury Chief Information Officer identified Treasury's Enterprise Identity, Credential and Access Management system as having scheduling problems. Since 2007, Treasury spent approximately $178 million to implement the requirements of Homeland Security Presidential Directive 12 for a common identity standard. Treasury received funding of $69 million in 2013 and is requesting a budget of $66 million in 2014. The implementation is targeted for completion in 2018.

We plan to determine if sound project management principles are being followed in carrying out the project.

Audit of Treasury's Controls over Implementation of Sequestration

On March 1, 2013, the President issued a sequestration order to executive departments and agencies canceling $85 billion in budgetary resources for fiscal year 2013 across the federal government in accordance with Section 251A of the Balanced Budget and Emergency Deficit Control Act of 1985, as Amended. The order required that budgetary resources in each non-exempt budget account be reduced by the amount calculated by OMB. OMB reported this amount in its report to Congress dated March 1, 2013, *OMB Report to the Congress on the Joint Committee Sequestration for FY 2013*. The report provided calculations of the percentages and amounts by which various budgetary resources are required to be reduced, and a listing of the reductions required for each non-exempt budget account. In addition, heads of executive departments and agencies received guidance memoranda from the President on planning for uncertainty with respect to fiscal year 2013 budgetary resources; and on agency responsibilities for implementation of sequestration.

We plan to determine if Treasury has (1) implemented management controls to achieve funding reductions due to sequestration and (2) implemented risk management strategies and internal controls that provide heightened scrutiny of certain types of activities funded from sequestered accounts including hiring, issuing discretionary monetary awards to employees, and incurring obligations for training, conferences, and travel.

Audit Resolution and Follow-Up

We plan to determine if Treasury's audit follow-up system is effective to ensure that audit recommendations are promptly and properly acted upon and that progress on corrective actions is adequately monitored. This project is intended to complement our corrective action verifications on specific audits. As part of this audit, we plan to follow up on our recommendations in *General Management: Office of Management Needs to Improve Its Monitoring of the Department's Audit Follow-up Process*, (OIG-08-037; June 23, 2008).

Conversion to Concur Travel System

BFS' Administrative Resource Center awarded a contract to Concur Technologies, Inc. and began implementation activities in January 2013 with a pilot planned for the spring. Concur Travel System (Concur) will replace GovTrip and will provide integrated travel and expense management solutions and manage online bookings, travel authorizations and voucher processing for Treasury agencies and bureaus. Concur is expected to help Treasury agencies realize the cost savings, compliance benefits, and reporting capabilities that arise from using an integrated travel and expense service and reduce operating costs over the next 15 years.

We plan to determine if sound project management principles are being followed in carrying out this project.

Resolution of Accountable Officer Irregularities

Accountable officers include certifying officers, disbursing officers, collecting officials, and other officers or employees who are responsible for or have custody of public funds. Treasury Directive 32-04, Settlement of Accounts and Relief of Accountable Officers, established the policy and procedures to settle irregularities (erroneous or improper payments) in the accounts of accountable officers. Requests for relief of accountable officers from liability for irregularities constituting a major loss must be referred to Treasury's Deputy Chief Financial Officer for resolution, except for requests for relief of BFS accountable officers with government-wide fiscal responsibilities, who must be referred to the Fiscal Assistant Secretary for resolution. The resolution of irregularities constituting a minor loss has been delegated to other Treasury officials.

We plan to determine if irregularities in the accounts of Treasury accountable officers are resolved in accordance with Treasury Directive 32-04.

Projects Under Consideration for Future Fiscal Years

Classification of Treasury Information

The 9/11 Commission and others observed that the over-classification of information interferes with accurate, actionable, and timely information sharing, increases the cost of information security, and needlessly limits stakeholder and public access to information. Over-classification of information causes considerable confusion over what information may be shared and with whom, and negatively affects the dissemination of information within the federal government and others. The Reducing Over-Classification Act requires the inspector general of each department or agency with an officer or employee who is authorized to make original classifications, in consultation with the Information Security Oversight Office, to carry out no less than two evaluations of that department or agency's classification policies, procedures, rules, and regulations by September 30, 2016. The first evaluation was required by September 30, 2013, and we plan to complete the second evaluation in 2016.

Consistent with the act, we plan to (1) assess whether applicable classification policies, procedures, rules, and regulations have been adopted, followed, and effectively administered within Treasury and (2) identify policies, procedures, rules, regulations, or management practices that may be contributing to persistent misclassification of material within Treasury.

Physical Access Controls Over Treasury Facilities

We plan to determine if sufficient protections exist to prevent unauthorized access into Treasury facilities.

Security Controls Over Forfeited Property

The Treasury Executive Office for Asset Forfeiture manages the Treasury Forfeiture Fund. Forfeited general property, vessels, aircraft, and vehicles are stored at warehouse locations across the U.S. and are managed by a contractor. The stored property is either sold, destroyed, or equitably shared with law enforcement agencies.

We plan to assess the security controls over forfeited property stored in contractor facilities.

Management of the National Seized Property Contract

The Treasury Executive Office for Asset Forfeiture administers the Treasury Forfeiture Fund, the receipt account for the deposit of nontax forfeitures made by Treasury and certain other federal law enforcement agencies. In 2007, the Treasury Executive Office for Asset Forfeiture contracted with VSE Corporation for general property services in support of the Treasury Forfeiture Fund's mission.

We plan to determine if the contracting actions and practices for the national seized property contract complied with policies, procedures, and guidelines established under the federal and Treasury acquisition requirements.

Employee Bonus Policies at Nonappropriated Bureaus

We plan to determine if nonappropriated bureaus have (1) established policies for employee bonuses in accordance with applicable laws and regulations and (2) paid bonuses in compliance with applicable laws, regulations, and policy and procedures. Separate audits are planned at each nonappropriated bureau.

Strategic Human Capital Management

We plan to determine if the Office of the Deputy Assistant Secretary for Human Resources and Chief Human Capital Officer identified any existing critical skill gaps at Treasury and modified its strategic human capital management plan accordingly.

PortfolioStat

The Administration's Campaign to Cut Waste directed agencies to seek opportunities to shift to commodity IT, leverage technology, procurement, and best practices government-wide; and build on existing investments. In October 2011, OMB launched the Shared First Initiative aimed at reducing waste and duplication across the federal IT portfolio. In order to implement these initiatives, agencies are to review their respective IT investment portfolios to identify opportunities to consolidate the acquisition and management of commodity IT services, and increase the use of shared-service delivery models. To support this process, OMB issued Memorandum M-12-11, *Implementing PortfolioStat,* in March 2012 to require agency chief operating officers to annually lead an agency-wide IT portfolio review within their respective organization.

We plan to assess Treasury's implementation of PortfolioStat.

Mandated Reports

We plan to determine if Treasury has adequate monitoring controls in place to ensure the completion of presidentially and congressionally mandated reports. As part of this project, we will assess Treasury's progress to reduce, eliminate, or consolidate reports pursuant to the Government Performance and Results Modernization Act.

Supply Chain Security

We will determine if Treasury's acquisition process has incorporated steps to mitigate supply-chain threats to computer hardware and software procured for its use.

Treasury's Environmental and Sustainability Program

We plan to determine Treasury's compliance with applicable laws, regulations, executive orders, and agency directives with respect to managing its environmental programs and climate change. As part of this work, we will assess Treasury's progress towards meeting it sustainability goals identified in its *Strategic Sustainability Performance Plan*.

Work Life Programs

We plan to determine if Treasury tracks and evaluates data on the implementation and assessment of its work-life programs.

Telework Program Oversight

We plan to determine if Treasury and non-IRS bureaus have policies, procedures, and controls over employee telework.

Website Compliance with Section 508 of the Rehabilitation Act

Section 508 of the Rehabilitation Act of 1973, as amended, contains accessibility requirements for federal departments and agencies that develop, procure, maintain, or use electronic and information technology. The purpose of Section 508 is to ensure that individuals with disabilities have access to and use of information and data in electronic or IT format—regardless of the type of medium of the technology—that is comparable to the access to and use of the information and data by members of the public who do not have disabilities.

We plan to determine if Treasury's website and its bureaus conform to the technical standards of Section 508 for web-based intranet and internet information.

Review of Treasury International Capital Reporting System

The Treasury International Capital (TIC) reporting system collects data for the United States on cross-border portfolio investment flows and positions between U.S. residents (including U.S.-based branches of firms headquartered in other countries) and foreign residents (including offshore branches of U.S. firms).

This system provides:

- monthly data on transactions in long-term securities;
- monthly and quarterly position data on claims and liabilities (including some short-term securities) reported by banks and broker/dealers of securities;
- quarterly position data on selected claims and liabilities reported by non-banks and non-broker/dealers;
- annual position data on holdings of long-term and short-term securities; and
- quarterly position and transactions data on financial derivatives.

Besides being reported on the TIC website, detailed data from the monthly and quarterly TIC forms are combined and presented in several tables in the Capital Movements section of the quarterly Treasury Bulletin. TIC reporting system data, including the data from the periodic surveys of holdings of securities, are also a primary input to the Bureau of Economic Analysis' International Transactions Accounts and for the International Investment Position of the United States. The TIC reporting system data is indirectly the basis of the Federal Reserve's Flow of Funds accounts for financial positions and flows of the Rest of the World sector. The Flow of Funds accounts use as their primary input the data as published by Bureau of Economic Analysis in its international transactions accounts, which is based on the TIC reporting system data. The TIC reporting system data is also used to compute the U.S. Gross External Debt position, which is published as part of the International Monetary Fund's Special Data Dissemination Standard.

We plan to (1) review the data in the TIC reporting system for reliability and completeness; (2) review the process for accumulating data in the TIC reporting system for compliance with applicable procedures, policies, regulations or laws; and (3) determine if controls are in place to safeguard financial data and any sensitive information in the TIC reporting system.

Treasury's Enterprise Architecture Program

We plan to determine if Treasury complies with established federal guidance and Treasury's enterprise architecture policies and procedures, and to determine if the Treasury aligned its strategic plans and individual business priorities within an appropriate enterprise architecture framework.

Contractor Clearance and Background Investigation

We plan to determine if controls are in place to ensure that Treasury's contractor personnel who have access to Treasury data and other information have current and appropriate security clearances and background investigations.

Employee Background Investigations

We plan to determine if controls are in place to ensure that Treasury employee background investigations and re-investigations are timely.

Audit of Treasury's Email Electronic Records Management Practices

The media has reported that U.S. government officials have used private email and alias accounts to conduct official government business. The use of these accounts could seriously impair records collection, preservation, and access, therefore compromising transparency and oversight. The Federal Records Act requires agency heads to make and preserve records containing adequate and proper documentation of the organization, functions, policies, decisions, procedures, and essential transactions of the agency.

We plan to identify the use by Treasury, if any, of private and alias email accounts to conduct official business, and assess the controls over such accounts to ensure compliance with federal records retention requirements.

Treasury's Management of Facilities

The federal government is the biggest property owner in the U.S. The President proposed a Civilian Property Realignment Board to sell or get rid of property it no longer needs. The Presidential Memorandum, *Disposing of Unneeded Real Estate,* dated June 10, 2010, required federal agencies to save no less than $3 billion by the end of fiscal year 2012. Treasury reported savings of $24 million in real property cost savings through fiscal year 2012. On May 11, 2012, OMB issued Memorandum M-12-12, Promoting Efficient Spending to Support Agency Operations, which prevents agencies from increasing square footage and requires agency reporting on real property.

We plan to assess Treasury's effort to implement the President's Memorandum and the OMB memorandum.

Survey of Treasury's Human Resource Succession Planning

We plan to determine if Treasury established human resource succession plans.

Treasury Secure Data Network Project Management

We plan to determine if (1) the project business case for upgrading and enhancing the Treasury Secure Data Network, a classified communications system, is based on appropriate assumptions and cost/benefit estimates and (2) sound project management principles are followed in carrying out the project.

Capital Planning and Investment Control Process

We plan to assess Treasury's management of its capital planning and investment process for IT projects.

Treasury's Performance Data

The Government Performance and Results Act of 1993, as amended by the Government Performance and Results Modernization Act of 2010, requires the Department to establish performance measures for its programs. These performance measures are published annually in the

Department's Annual Performance Report. Performance measure data is reported to the Department's Office of Performance and Budget by individual component entities.

We plan to review the Department's process to accumulate and report performance data and determine if select performance data reported in the Annual Performance Report is supported.

FOIA Requests

We plan to determine if the Department and non-IRS bureaus (1) have adequate systems to record, track, and timely complete FOIA requests; (2) provide points of contact and monitoring systems to ensure that inquiries regarding existing requests have been properly addressed with the requesters; (3) ensure proper collection of fees and the granting of fee waivers; and (4) ensure compliance with the 2011 Supreme Court decision Milner v. Department of the Navy, and the 1996 electronic FOIA amendments, and (5) report required FOIA statistics annually to the Department of Justice.

Terrorist Financing, Money Laundering, and Foreign Assets Control

Issue Area Discussion

Preventing terrorism, money laundering, and other criminal activity is a global effort. Treasury's role in this effort is to safeguard the U.S. financial system and protect it from illicit use. Treasury coordinates with other law enforcement agencies, intelligence agencies, foreign governments, and the private sector to add transparency to the financial system to more easily detect those who would try to exploit the financial system for their own illicit purposes. Within Treasury, this effort is led by the Office of Terrorism and Financial Intelligence. The office oversees the Office of Terrorist Financing and Financial Crime, Office of Intelligence and Analysis, FinCEN, and the Office of Foreign Assets Control (OFAC). The Office of Terrorist Financing and Financial Crime manages the Office of Terrorism and Financial Intelligence policy and outreach. The Office of Intelligence and Analysis is responsible for intelligence functions, integrating Treasury into the larger intelligence community, and providing support to Treasury leadership. FinCEN is responsible for Treasury's effort to enforce the Bank Secrecy Act (BSA) and the USA PATRIOT Act. OFAC administers laws that impose economic sanctions against hostile targets to further U.S. foreign policy and national security objectives.

BSA requires financial institutions to file Currency Transaction Reports for cash transactions exceeding $10,000 and Suspicious Activity Reports for transactions that are suspicious in nature. Law enforcement uses these reports to identify and guard against fraud, money laundering, terrorist financing, and other types of illicit finance. FinCEN has focused efforts in recent years on improving and increasing electronic filing of these reports. FinCEN is also implementing a BSA IT Modernization program that will re-engineer BSA data architecture, update the infrastructure, implement more innovative web services and enhanced electronic filing, and provide analytical tools. FinCEN plans to complete BSA IT Modernization in 2014.

Title III of the USA PATRIOT Act requires each financial institution to establish an anti-money laundering (AML) program, extends the Suspicious Activity Report filing requirement to broker-dealers, requires financial institutions to establish procedures to verify the identities and addresses of customers seeking to open accounts, and requires FinCEN to maintain a highly secure network that allows financial institutions to file BSA reports electronically. Beginning April 1, 2013, financial institutions must use new FinCEN forms for the Suspicious Activity Report, Currency Transaction Report, Registration for Money Services Businesses, and Designation Of Exempt Person reports, which are available only electronically through the BSA E-Filing System. Financial institutions that continue to file mandated reports in paper format will fail to meet BSA reporting requirements and may be subject to civil money penalties.

To better share information and improve coordination in ensuring that BSA is effectively implemented, FinCEN has a memorandum of understanding with the federal banking agencies—

OCC, Federal Deposit Insurance Corporation (FDIC), FRB, and the National Credit Union Administration—and similar memoranda of understanding with IRS and most states and territories. FinCEN also has memoranda of understanding with the Securities and Exchange Commission and the Commodity Futures Trading Commission to enhance BSA compliance oversight in the nonbank financial sectors.

OFAC's authority to impose controls on transactions and to freeze foreign assets is derived from the President's constitutional and statutory wartime and national emergency powers. OFAC relies principally on authority under the Trading with the Enemy Act, International Emergency Economic Powers Act, and the United Nations Participation Act to prohibit or regulate commercial or financial transactions involving specific foreign countries, entities, or individuals. OFAC works with other federal agencies to implement and enforce these programs. Like FinCEN, OFAC executed a memorandum of understanding with the federal banking agencies to share information and improve coordination.

In September 2010, FinCEN proposed a regulatory requirement for financial institutions to report cross-border electronic transmittals of funds. If implemented, such a requirement has the potential to greatly assist law enforcement in detecting transnational organized crime, multinational drug cartels, terrorist financing, and international tax evasion according to FinCEN. Implementation is dependent on completion of the BSA IT Modernization program. While we do not have any specific proposals related to this initiative in this annual plan, we will monitor the area for planning future work.

Under a new director for fiscal year 2013, FinCEN reorganized its functions.

Areas of Concern

Terrorism, narcotics trafficking, human smuggling and trafficking, loan modification and foreclosure scams, mortgage fraud, health care fraud, and other organized criminal activity remain as high level concerns for the U.S. These activities all involve movement of funds and use of financial systems. Continued instability in the Middle East remains a significant challenge. In North America, increasing drug smuggling and violence related to drug cartels in Mexico have increased smuggling, crime, and violence along our Southern Border. The financial crisis resulted in increased mortgage fraud and loan modification scams. Law enforcement continues to target organizations and individuals involved in defrauding the Medicare and Medicaid programs.

Over the last decade, the U.S. and others in the global community have required increased reporting and monitoring of financial institution transactions. In reaction to the activities largely occurring in the Middle East, including the nuclear development activities in Iran, the U.S. increased sanctions on transactions involving countries in these areas. Because terrorists and criminals are resourceful and cunning, they are reacting to the increase in financial institution monitoring by looking for ways of moving funds to support their illicit activity that more easily avoid detection. This includes, among other things, the use of electronic transactions (online and mobile) and prepaid instruments that make it increasingly difficult for financial institutions and law enforcement to detect illicit transactions, and the use of the nonbank financial sector where there is likely to be less monitoring and more opportunity to hide transactions, including money services businesses and informal value transfer systems. Most recently FinCEN has focused its attention on codifying, clarifying, and strengthening existing customer due diligence regulatory requirements and supervisory expectations primarily for banks, brokers or dealers in securities, mutual funds, futures commission merchants, and brokers in commodities. The purpose was to enhance identification and verification of accountholders and beneficial ownership which is any individual or group of individuals that, either directly or indirectly, has the power to vote or influence transaction decisions. The risk is that nominal account holders can enable individuals and business entities to conceal the identity of the true owner of assets or property derived from or associated with criminal activity.

Anti-money laundering andcombating financing of terrorists remains a high priority. Our prior audits have revealed problems pertaining to the detection of BSA violations, the timely enforcement of BSA, Suspicious Activity Report data quality, BSA system development efforts, and administration of sanctions. Moreover, the universe of institutions required to comply with BSA requirements has grown as nonbank financial institutions participate in the program. The universe now includes the insurance industry and precious stones and metals dealers.

Potential Integrity Risks

Treasury efforts to support law enforcement in the fight against terrorist financing, money laundering, and other financial crimes are dependent on honest and complete reporting of currency transactions and suspicious financial activity. Potential integrity risks include (1) the failure by financial institutions to file required BSA reports, due to both poorly run programs and corrupt bank officials who are involved in the schemes; (2) filing of false or fraudulent BSA reports; (3) internal and external misuse or disclosure of sensitive BSA information contrary to law; and (4) inappropriate handling or use of sensitive but unclassified, law enforcement–sensitive, or classified information.

In-Progress and Planned Fiscal Year 2014 Projects

FinCEN BSA IT Modernization Program (Ongoing)

Pursuant to a Congressional directive, we are conducting a series of audits to determine if FinCEN is (1) meeting cost, schedule, and performance benchmarks for the BSA IT Modernization program, and (2) providing appropriate contractor oversight. We will report on these objectives every 6 months until the system development is completed, which is expected in 2014.

FinCEN Efforts to Ensure Compliance by MSBs With BSA (In-Progress)

In 2005, our office issued an audit report recommending that FinCEN take actions to improve the registration program for Money Service Businesses (MSB). Registration is the first and vital step in (1) identifying possible money laundering and terrorist financing, often perpetrated by unlicensed and unregistered MSBs; (2) performing appropriate BSA examinations and monitoring filings of suspicious activity reports; (3) monitoring compliance with OFAC sanctions; and (4) taking enforcement actions for BSA or OFAC violations. In 2009 and 2010, FinCEN issued proposed rules to tighten emerging threats associated with activities that often involve MSBs. These include rules to more clearly delineate the scope of entities regulated as MSBs and tightening rules associated with MSBs, which are difficult to enforce. These rules govern the use of prepaid access cards and the reporting of cross-border wire transfers. FinCEN also issued an advisory regarding the use of informal value transfer systems by unlicensed and unregistered MSBs, citing several which had been involved in money laundering or violations of OFAC sanctions.

We plan to assess whether FinCEN has taken sufficient action, in response to our 2005 report to establish adequate management systems and controls over MSB registration and BSA compliance.

OFAC Licensing Programs (In-Progress)

We plan to determine (1) the universe of licensing programs under OFAC's jurisdiction; (2) the related laws, regulations, and OFAC's policies and procedures for these programs; and (3) whether the programs are administered in an appropriate manner.

OFAC Libyan Sanctions Case Study (In-Progress)

The President issued E.O. 13566 on February 25, 2011, blocking property and prohibiting certain transactions related to Libya in order to protect Libyan state assets from misappropriation. This order was issued based on findings that Colonel Muammar Qadhafi, his government, and close associates, have taken extreme measures against the people of Libya, including using weapons of war, mercenaries, and wanton violence against unarmed civilians. By March 1, 2011, Treasury reported at least $30 billion in Government of Libya assets were frozen under the E.O. The reported amount of frozen Libyan assets increased to approximately $37 billion by September 2011. In an effort to return the frozen assets to the Libyan people, on September 1, 2011, OFAC released an initial $700 million in frozen assets to the Libyan Transitional National Council for fuel and civilian operating costs and to pay salaries in support of the Libyan people. Treasury announced that going forward; it would remain in close contact with the council for the release of additional assets. On December 16, 2011, the U.S. unfroze all Libyan government and Central Bank funds within U.S. jurisdiction, with limited exceptions. Only those assets in the U.S. of the Qadhafi family and former members of the former Qadhafi regime remain frozen.

We plan to perform a case study on OFAC's implementation and subsequent lifting of most of the sanctions against Libya. For the purpose of this project, we plan to (1) review OFAC's implementation of the Libyan sanctions program; (2) determine how frozen assets are identified, maintained, and accounted for; (3) review OFAC's subsequent and gradual release of frozen Libyan assets; and (4) determine how OFAC will identify and release all frozen assets to their rightful owners upon termination of the sanctions program.

OCC's BSA and USA PATRIOT Act Compliance Examinations and Enforcement Actions (In-Progress)

We plan to determine the effectiveness of OCC's programs to conduct supervisory activities and, when necessary, take enforcement actions to ensure that national banks have controls in place and provide the requisite notices to law enforcement to deter and detect money laundering, terrorist financing, and other related criminal acts. The scope of this review will include OCC's examination coverage of BSA compliance by former thrifts supervised by the former Office of Thrift Supervision (OTS), which were transferred to OCC in July 2011. Additionally, the scope of this review will include national bank trust departments and banks offering both private banking services and correspondent bank accounts (which make payments or handle transactions on behalf of a foreign bank).

Treasury Executive Office of Asset Forfeiture's Use of Treasury Forfeiture Fund Receipts to Support Law Enforcement (In-Progress)

We plan to determine if the Treasury Executive Office of Asset Forfeiture has appropriate controls to (1) award and distribute funds to eligible law enforcement agencies in accordance with applicable laws, regulations, and policies and (2) ensure that distributed receipts are used for intended purposes. As part of this work, we plan to determine if selected state and local government agencies use Treasury forfeiture funds in accordance with Treasury guidelines.

FinCEN Implementation of USA PATRIOT Act Information-Sharing Procedures (In-Progress)

The USA PATRIOT Act provides for the sharing of information between the government and financial institutions, and among financial institutions regarding individuals, entities, and organizations engaged in or reasonably suspected of engaging in terrorist acts or money laundering activities. In March 2005, FinCEN implemented a web-based secure communications system to expedite sharing of this information.

We plan to determine the extent to which information sharing is occurring among the government and financial institutions.

Financial Institution Filing of Reports to OFAC and FinCEN on Blocked Transactions (In-Progress)

In December 2004, FinCEN advised institutions subject to BSA suspicious activity reporting that under certain circumstances reports filed with OFAC related to blocked transactions with designated terrorists, foreign terrorist organizations, and narcotics traffickers and trafficker kingpins would fulfill the requirement to file suspicious activity reports with FinCEN (i.e., a separate suspicious activity report to FinCEN on the same blocked transaction would no longer be required). However, if the institution has information not included on the blocking report filed with OFAC, a suspicious activity report containing that information must still be filed with FinCEN.

We plan to determine if OFAC and FinCEN implemented controls to ensure that the information in reports filed with OFAC on blocked transactions is made available to law enforcement through FinCEN databases as appropriate.

FinCEN Civil Penalties for BSA Program Violations

We plan to determine FinCEN's process for assessing and collecting civil penalties when BSA violations occur.

OCC's Implementation of the Permanent Subcommittee on Investigation's Recommendations in Response to the HSBC Case

In July 2012, the Permanent Subcommittee on Investigations of the Senate Committee on Homeland Security and Governmental Affairs reported that lax oversight by top HSBC executives gave terrorists and drug cartels access to the U.S. financial system. The Subcommittee recommended OCC align its practice with that of other federal bank regulators by treating AML deficiencies as a safety and soundness matter, rather than a consumer compliance matter; establish a policy to conduct institution-wide examinations of bank AML programs, consider use of formal or informal enforcement actions to act on AML problems, and strengthen its AML examinations. In December 2012, HSBC agreed to pay $1.92 billion to settle money laundering and sanctions violations.

We plan to determine OCC's responses to each of the Subcommittee's recommendations and the status of OCC's efforts to implement the Subcommittee's recommendations.

FinCEN Reorganization

In February 2013, FinCEN's Director presented Congress with FinCEN's plan to reorganize. The plan included a reorganization of employees by job function instead of by stakeholder. The primary purpose of the reorganization was to promote information sharing and better serve FinCEN's customers-the financial, law enforcement and regulatory communities.

We plan to assess how FinCEN's reorganization plan addresses the needs of the financial, law enforcement, and regulatory communities.

FinCEN Efforts to Identify Fraud

We plan to survey FinCEN's efforts in proactively identifying potential healthcare, mortgage, insurance, and other frauds; and in disseminating that information to law enforcement and regulatory agencies. The survey results will be used to determine if more in-depth audit coverage of this area is warranted.

Responsibilities of the Office of Intelligence and Analysis under the Intelligence Authorization Act

The Intelligence Authorization Act for Fiscal Year 2004 established the Office of Intelligence and Analysis and assigned it responsibility for receiving, analyzing, collating, and disseminating foreign intelligence and foreign counterintelligence information related to Treasury operations.

We plan to assess the office's progress toward meeting its responsibilities.

FinCEN's Implementation of Section 311 of the USA PATRIOT Act

Section 311 of the USA Patriot Act grants the Secretary of the Treasury the authority to require domestic financial institutions to take certain special measures with respect to foreign jurisdictions, foreign financial institutions, classes of transactions, or types of accounts identified as primary money laundering concerns. The authority to propose and implement the special measures under Section 311 has been delegated by the Secretary to FinCEN. Special measures that may be implemented by FinCEN include recordkeeping and reporting on certain financial transactions, collecting information relating to certain accounts, and enforcing prohibitions or conditions on opening or maintaining certain accounts. Special measures are proposed by FinCEN through Notices of Proposed Rule Making. After comments received in response to Notices of Proposed Rule Making are reviewed and any other available information considered, FinCEN may promulgate final rules, withdraw the findings and proposed rules, or keep matters open for further review.

We plan to assess the mechanisms FinCEN has in place to implement actions under Section 311 of the USA Patriot Act.

FinCEN Rules for Filing the Report of Foreign Bank and Financial Accounts

Report of Foreign Bank and Financial Accounts(FBAR) is to be filed by persons in the United States who have a financial interest in or signature authority over at least one financial account located outside of the United States which exceeded $10,000 at any time during the calendar year. The FBAR is a tool to help the U.S. government identify persons who may be using foreign financial accounts to circumvent U.S. law. Several exemptions exist for certain individuals which have been questioned and required FinCEN to issue clarifying guidance.

We plan to determine if FinCEN is using FBARs in its analyses, and how the bureau has determined what exemptions are appropriate. We also plan to determine why FinCEN continues to extend the effective FBAR filing dates for certain individuals.

OFAC's Management of the Specially Designated Nationals and Blocked Persons List

OFAC is responsible for enforcing economic and trade sanctions against targeted foreign countries, terrorists, and international narcotics traffickers. A major component to these sanctions is the Specially Designated Nationals and Blocked Persons List, which includes over 3,500 names of individuals, governments, and companies that serve as agents or representatives of countries with which U.S. businesses and citizens are prohibited from engaging in trade. In consultation with the Departments of State and Justice, OFAC relies on both public and classified data to list an entity on the list. Entities who wish to challenge OFAC's designation can apply to OFAC for delisting, and must credibly demonstrate they no longer engage in or plan to engage in the sanctioned activity, and that the circumstances resulting in the designation no longer apply. Over the last 3 years, OFAC reported that it removed about 1,500 entities from the list and expects to remove at least 600 more by the end of 2013. In a related development, in June 2012, OFAC announced it launched a new Specially Designated Nationals data system.

We plan to determine and assess OFAC's management controls over the process of listing and delisting individuals and entities from the Specially Designated Nationals and Blocked Persons List and assess the effectiveness of the new data system in helping OFAC manage this process.

Terrorist Finance Tracking Program

After the terrorist attacks on September 11, 2001, Treasury initiated the Terrorist Finance Tracking Program to identify, track, and pursue terrorists and their networks. During 2010, the U.S. and the European Union entered into a new agreement on the transfer and processing of data in the Terrorist

Finance Tracking Program. As provided in the agreement, we will provide appropriate oversight of the program.

Follow-up on a Classified Program

We plan to follow-up on the implementation of recommendations made in an audit report of a classified program.

Treasury Executive Office for Asset Forfeiture's Controls over Super Surplus and the Secretary's Enforcement Fund

The Super Surplus Fund is a special receipt account, which means that the fund can be used to provide money to other federal entities toward the accomplishment of a specific objective for which the recipient bureaus are authorized to spend money toward other authorized expenses. In fiscal year 2012, $78.7 million in Super Surplus funds were expensed. The Secretary Enforcement Fund is available for federal law enforcement purposes of any Treasury law enforcement organization or law enforcement bureau that participates in the Fund. TEOAF is also responsible for determining how the Secretary Enforcement Fund funds are spent. In fiscal year 2012, the Fund expensed just over $9.5 million in Secretary Enforcement Funds.

We plan to determine the methodology TEOAF uses to award Super Surplus Fund and Secretary Enforcement Fund funds. We will also assess the controls TEOAF uses to monitor the use of monies obtained through the respective funds.

FinCEN's Guidance Electronic Currency and Prepaid Access

Electronic money is also known as e-money, e-currency, electronic cash, electronic currency, digital money, digital cash, digital currency, or cyber currency. Typically, e-money involves the use of computer networks, the internet and digital stored value systems. Electronic funds transfer, direct deposit, digital gold currency, and virtual currency are all examples of electronic money.

Digital currencies provide a potential money laundering instrument because they facilitate international payments without the transmittal services of traditional financial institutions. Prepaid access is defined as access to funds (or the future value of funds) that have been paid in advance and can be retrieved or transferred in the future through an electronic device or vehicle, such as a card, code, electronic serial number, mobile identification number, or personal identification number.

In July 2011, FinCEN issued a final rule to clarify the definition of prepaid access and impose suspicious activity reporting, customer identification, and recordkeeping requirements on both providers and sellers of prepaid access, and registration requirements on sellers. In March 2013, FinCEN issued *Application of FinCEN's Regulations to Persons Administering, Exchanging, or Using Virtual Currencies*. This interpretive guidance was issued to clarify the applicability of the regulations implementing the BSA to persons creating, obtaining, distributing, exchanging, accepting, or transmitting virtual currencies.

We plan to determine if FinCEN has provided timely and relevant guidance to monitor e-money products, including efforts to assess risks associated with mobile banking and prepaid access, and how FinCEN is addressing the vulnerabilities to the financial system with the use of these products.

Projects Under Consideration for Future Fiscal Years

OFAC's System Development Process

Prior OIG and GAO audits found OFAC's Administrative System for Investigations and Sanctions (OASIS) did not adequately record, track, and report licensing activities. Though the system has been upgraded several times since 2002, it still has not fully addressed all of OFAC's licensing needs. Additionally, OFAC has undertaken development of the Automated Blocked and Rejected Report System to provide the office with an electronic filing system to track the blocking of financial transactions involving entities or persons subject to OFAC sanctions. OFAC has consistently cited lack of funding and ongoing system security issues as the primary causes for hindering development of these systems.

We plan to evaluate OFAC's process for defining, designing, testing and implementing new software applications or programs for OASIS and the Automated Blocked and Rejected Report System to meet users' needs. We will also assess OFAC's oversight of its systems development process.

OFAC Civil Penalty Cases

OFAC enforces economic sanctions by issuing civil and criminal penalties. These penalties serve as a deterrent to acts that violate sanction programs. Past audits have revealed that some civil and criminal cases have not been acted upon in a timely fashion allowing them to fall out of the statute of limitations. If illegal acts go unpunished, this could result in more violations of foreign sanctions since there would be no consequence for not complying with these sanctions. In 2006, we reported that OFAC had allowed hundreds of enforcement cases to expire without issuing civil money penalties because of poor case management.

We plan to determine if OFAC has implemented case management processes for its civil and criminal penalty activities to ensure timely action is taken.

FinCEN's Oversight of BSA Examination and Enforcement for Nonbank Residential Mortgage Originators and Brokers

In February 2012, FinCEN issued final regulations requiring nonbank residential mortgage lenders and originators to establish anti-money laundering programs and file suspicious activity reports. FinCEN believes that the new regulations will help mitigate risks and minimize vulnerabilities that criminals have exploited in the nonbank residential mortgage sector.

We plan to evaluate FinCEN's strategy for establishing an examination and compliance program for nonbank mortgage originators and brokers.

FinCEN Memorandum of Understanding With Federal Banking Agencies

We plan to determine if (1) FinCEN is receiving timely, complete, and reliable information in accordance with the memorandum of understanding; and (2) the purpose of the memorandum of understanding, which was to enhance communication and coordination enabling financial institutions to identify, deter, and interdict terrorist financing and money laundering, is being achieved. We plan to conduct audit work at FinCEN and OCC.

OFAC Memorandum of Understanding With Federal Banking Agencies

We plan to determine (1) whether OFAC is receiving timely, complete, and reliable information under the April 2006 memorandum of understanding with federal banking agencies, and (2) if the memorandum of understanding is achieving its purpose of helping OFAC administer and enforce economic sanctions and assisting the federal banking agencies in fulfilling their roles as banking organization supervisors. We plan to conduct audit work at OFAC and OCC.

FinCEN's Analysis and Dissemination of Report of International Transportation of Currency or Monetary Instruments Data

In accordance with 31 U.S.C. 5316 (a), persons who physically transport, mail, or ship currency or other monetary instruments in an aggregate amount exceeding $10,000 at one time from the United States to any place outside the United States, or into the United States from any place outside the United States, is required to file a Currency or Monetary Instruments (CMIR), which is FinCEN Form 105, with Department of Homeland Security, Customs and Border Protection. These reports are useful for identifying money laundering schemes.

We plan to determine if FinCEN is analyzing CMIR data along with other BSA filings to prevent and detect money laundering schemes, and is coordinating with Customs and Border Protection. We will also determine how this information is shared with law enforcement and other regulatory agencies for their examination, compliance, and enforcement efforts.

Treasury's Compliance with Intelligence Reporting Requirements

E.O. 13462, *President's Intelligence Advisory Board and Intelligence Oversight Board,* as amended, requires Treasury to report intelligence gathering activities to the President's Intelligence Advisory Board and its component, the Intelligence Oversight Board. The President's Intelligence Advisory Board is responsible for keeping the President apprised of issues discovered through intelligence gathering activities throughout the federal government under E.O. 13462 and the *Criteria on Thresholds for Reporting Intelligence Oversight Matters and Instructions Relating to Formatting and Scheduling,* from the Office of the Director of National Intelligence. The Office of Intelligence and Analysis is responsible for submitting quarterly reports on intelligence activities that it has reason to believe may be unlawful or contrary to executive orders or Presidential directives. These reports are provided to the President's Intelligence Advisory Board and the Director of National Intelligence. This quarterly report also covers any matters considered significant or highly sensitive as defined under the criteria. The E.O. also requires Treasury to act on any recommendations made by the board and the Director of

National Intelligence, including instructions to discontinue activities that may be unlawful or contrary to executive orders or other Presidential directives.

We plan to determine if Treasury (1) established policies and procedures to meet the requirements of E.O. 13462; (2) submitted reports mandated by the President's Intelligence Advisory Board; and (3) if applicable, took appropriate actions when directed to by this Board or the Director of National Intelligence.

Office of Terrorist Financing and Financial Crimes Interagency Collaboration with the National Security Community

The Office of Terrorist Financing and Financial Crimes develops initiatives and deploys strategies to combat money laundering, terrorist financing, weapons of mass destruction proliferation, and other criminal and illicit activities, both domestically and abroad. This effort requires the Office of Terrorist Financing and Financial Crimes to work among the national security community, including the law enforcement, regulatory, policy, diplomatic and intelligence communities as well as with the private sector and foreign governments in order to identify and address threats of illicit finance to the international financial system.

We plan to assess the Office of Terrorist Financing and Financial Crimes' collaboration with the national security community, including the law enforcement, regulatory, policy, diplomatic and intelligence communities as well as with the private sector and foreign governments to identify and address threats of illicit finance to the international financial system.

FinCEN's Efforts to Ensure BSA Compliance by Nonbank Financial Institutions

FinCEN has the responsibility for oversight of the BSA for nonbank financial institutions which do not have a federal functional regulator. FinCEN delegated examination authority for these institutions to IRS. In an effort to better leverage examination resources, FinCEN is looking also to coordinate with the states.

We plan to determine how FinCEN is ensuring that nonbank institutions are compliant with the BSA.

FinCEN's Resource Center Regulatory Helpline

FinCEN's Resource Center Regulatory Helpline (helpline) provides regulatory assistance for financial institutions seeking clarification of their obligations under BSA and certain requirements under the USA PATRIOT Act. FinCEN's goal is to provide financial institutions with understandable guidance so that they can establish appropriate AML programs that comply with FinCEN's regulations. FinCEN's Helpline faces many competing demands.

We plan to assess FinCEN's helpline in providing assistance to the financial community to meet obligations under the BSA and USA Patriot Act.

Disposition of Forfeited Property

We plan to evaluate the Treasury Forfeiture Fund's controls over the disposition of forfeited property. In addition, we will determine if the property contractor is disposing of property in compliance with the terms of the contract.

Impact of FinCEN's Rules on Financial Institutions Subject to the Comprehensive Iran Sanctions, Accountability, and Divestment Act

The Comprehensive Iran Sanctions, Accountability, and Divestment Act of 2010 imposed sanctions aimed at persuading the Iranian government to end its illicit nuclear program. The financial sanctions prescribed by the act were designed to restrict or prohibit U.S. financial institutions from doing business with foreign institutions related to or conducting business with the government of Iran or its agents. Under the act, FinCEN was authorized to require U.S. banks to perform sanctions audits on foreign financial institutions with which they keep correspondent accounts to determine if those institutions are in compliance with requirements of the act. FinCEN issued the final rule in October 2011.

We plan to assess FinCEN's efforts to ensure financial institution compliance with the final rule.

Government-wide Financial Services and Debt Management

Issue Area Discussion

In October 2012, BPD and FMS began consolidating operations, becoming BFS. Treasury expects the consolidation to improve the delivery of public service, reduce the footprint of the federal government, and manage administrative and IT costs. The consolidation is intended to allow BFS to take advantage of economies of scale, eliminate overlapping and duplicative functions, and reduce administrative overhead and support services costs. In addition, it plans to consolidate its payment centers from four to two in fiscal year 2014. Treasury estimates that BFS will have 278 fewer full-time equivalent employees in 2014 than 2013 and a smaller budget by $0.4 million. The consolidation is expected to be completed in fiscal year 2020.

Treasury, through BFS, borrows the money needed to operate the federal government, accounts for the resulting debt, and provides reimbursable support services to federal agencies. The goal of Treasury debt management is to achieve the lowest borrowing costs over time by committing to regular and predictable debt issuance.

The federal debt has two major components: Debt Held by the Public and Intragovernmental Holdings. Debt Held by the Public is the debt held by individuals, corporations, state or local governments, foreign governments, and other entities outside the U.S. government. Types of securities held by the public include Treasury Bills, Treasury Notes, Treasury Bonds, Treasury Inflation-Protected Securities, U.S. Savings Bonds, State and Local Government Series Securities, Foreign Series securities, and Domestic Series securities. Intragovernmental Holdings are primarily Government Account Series securities held by federal government trust funds, revolving funds, and special funds. As of June 30, 2013, the total federal debt outstanding was $16.7 trillion, of which $11.9 trillion was Debt Held by the Public and $4.8 trillion was Intragovernmental Holdings. The interest expense on the federal debt for fiscal year 2012 was $359.8 billion. Interest expense for fiscal year 2013, as of June 30, 2013, was $345.3 billion. BFS' debt operations depend on modernized electronic and information system technology. Implemented by BPD in 2002, the TreasuryDirect system maintains approximately 1.3 million accounts.

BFS also provides central payment services to federal agencies, operates the federal government's collections and deposit systems, provides government-wide accounting and reporting services (including preparation of the Financial Report of the United States Government), and manages collection of delinquent debt owed the federal government.

One of BFS' primary goals is to provide reliable and accurate processing of federal payments, which is an essential part of supporting the U.S. economy. These payments total over $2.4 trillion annually. BFS issues over a billion payments a year by paper check, electronic funds transfer, and Fedwire. BFS has increased its efforts to make payments electronically, thereby reducing the number of paper checks issued. As of May 2012, approximately 80 percent of Social Security recipients receive benefits electronically. BFS also collects approximately $3.1 trillion a year through approximately 10,000 financial institutions. Nearly $2.9 trillion of this amount is collected electronically. Since enactment of the Debt Collection Improvement Act of 1996, Treasury, through BFS, collected about $62 billion in delinquent federal nontax debt. In fiscal year 2012, BFS collected $2.4 billion of delinquent federal nontax debt. Prompt referral of eligible delinquent debts to Treasury by federal program agencies is critical to the success of collection efforts.

Do Not Pay Initiative

In E.O. 13520, *Reducing Improper Payments and Eliminating Waste in Federal Programs* (November 2009), the President directed agencies to identify ways in which information sharing may improve eligibility verification and pre-payment scrutiny. The President directed the establishment of a "single point of entry" through which agencies would access relevant data in order to determine eligibility for a federal award or payment. In an April 2012 memorandum, OMB described the efforts of OMB and Treasury to establish the Do Not Pay (DNP) Initiative. The memorandum directed agencies to develop a plan for using the DNP system for pre-payment eligibility reviews. In January 2013, IPERIA was enacted, codifying the ongoing efforts to develop and enhance the DNP Initiative. Additionally, IPERIA required that not later than June 1, 2013, all agencies review all payments and awards for all programs through the system established by OMB. As the federal government takes these important steps to prevent waste, fraud, and abuse in federal spending, it is vital for agencies to ensure that individual privacy is fully protected.

The DNP Initiative includes multiple resources that are designed to help agencies confirm that the right recipient obtains the right payment for the right reason at the right time. IPERIA provides the federal government with new tools and authorities to help agencies effectively implement the DNP Initiative. IPERIA also establishes new standards and procedures that apply to computer matching programs that are conducted for purposes of the DNP Initiative. As required by IPERIA, OMB is to issue guidance implementing the relevant parts of the law. In particular, the statute asks OMB to provide guidance to agencies on reimbursement of costs between agencies, retention and timely destruction of records, and prohibiting the duplication and redisclosure of records. Furthermore, IPERIA asks OMB to provide new guidance to help improve the effectiveness and responsiveness of agencies' Data Integrity Boards.[2]

The Do No Pay Business Center is a Treasury program designed to give critical information to paying agencies to help reduce improper payments. The Do Not Pay Business Center provides two services to agencies: the Do Not Pay Portal and Do Not Pay Data Analytics Service. Each agency can choose to use any combination of these DNP services in order to best meet their needs. The Do Not Pay Portal provides users with a single entry point to search for entities that may be listed in a variety of data sources such as: the List of Excluded Individuals/Entities, Social Security Administration's

---

[2] A board of senior personnel designated by the head of an agency that is responsible for reviewing the agency's proposals to conduct or participate in a matching program and for conducting an annual review of all matching programs in which the agency has participated.

Death Master File, Central Contractor Registry, Excluded Parties List System, and Debt Check. Three types of searches will be available so agencies can customize use of the portal to align with their business needs: online, batch, and continuous monitoring.

With its potential to significantly reduce improper payments while at the same time ensuring appropriate privacy, we anticipate that our office will need to provide significant resources to oversee Treasury's responsibilities under the DNP Initiative going forward.

Potential Integrity Risks

Integrity risks associated with government-wide financial services and debt management, affecting BFS include fraud and abuse by means of (1) unauthorized access to sensitive information, (2) filing false applications and claims, (3) providing false statements to obtain federal assistance or funds, (4) diversion of benefit proceeds, (5) check forgery, (6) promised services not delivered, and (7) misuse and mismanagement of federal funds. Furthermore, program risks related to this issue area include the inability to collect debt, inability to recover in a disaster, misallocation of program costs, and disruption of the federal payment function and service to the public. The changing nature of crime and recent technological innovations require that law enforcement look for and implement new ways to identify and prevent future criminal activities.

To minimize potential integrity risks, OIG plans to explore the use of data-mining methods to analyze BFS payments to reveal hidden patterns relating to trends, relationships, and correlations between the data. These data-mining methods have the potential to reveal trends and patterns that could identify ongoing fraud and abuse directed against or occurring within BFS.

In-Progress and Planned Fiscal Year 2014 Projects

Controls Over the Debit Card Program for Social Security and Other Federal Benefits (In-Progress)

BFS manages a debit card program to provide unbanked federal benefit recipients the option of receiving their federal benefit payments via a debit card. The Direct Express Debit Card Program is operated by Comerica and provides an electronic funds transfer alternative for unbanked Social Security and Supplemental Security Income and other federal beneficiaries.

We plan to determine whether controls related to debit card recipient data are adequate and whether sound acquisition to select the financial agent practices were followed.

Controls Over Routing Transit Numbers (In-Progress)

FRB establishes and assigns routing transit numbers to federal agencies, including Treasury.

We plan to determine if internal controls over the use of the routing transit numbers assigned to BFS prevent and detect misuse of these numbers.

Administrative Resource Center's Operational Independence (In-Progress)

The BFS Administrative Resource Center's mission is to provide administrative support—including accounting, travel, personnel management, and procurement services—to various federal agencies.

The Administrative Resource Center operates as a franchise fund and therefore does not receive appropriated funds. Instead, it charges customers for services provided. As of July 2013, the Administrative Resource Center had 18 Treasury customers and 67 non-Treasury customers.

We plan to determine if the Administrative Resource Center has internal controls to ensure operational independence from BFS funding.

Do Not Pay Program Implementation (In Progress)

We plan to assess the Do Not Pay Business Center's role in assisting federal agencies in reducing improper payments, to include the Center's efforts to assist agency IPERIA compliance.

BPD and FMS Consolidation (In-Progress)

We will determine if Treasury has a comprehensive plan to accomplish the consolidation and re-designation of BPD and FMS as BFS and determine how well Treasury followed its plan. We will also determine the reliability of projected cost savings resulting from the consolidation.

Use of Permanent and Indefinite Appropriation Funds

We plan to determine if selected permanent and indefinite appropriation funds at BFS are used in accordance with the underlying legislation.

Direct Express Debit Card Call Center Service

We plan to assess call center performance under the financial agency agreement, including the reliability of performance data provided by the financial agent.

Direct Express Debit Card Fees

The financial agent for the Direct Express Debit Card Program is allowed to assess certain fees to cardholders. We plan to perform a case study of the impact of the fees on individual cardholders.

Use of Beneficiary Data

We plan to assess controls that prevent financial agents from using customer data obtained through their activities under financial agent agreements to market other financial products.

Survey of Debt Check Program

Debt Check is an internet-based system intended to assist agencies with preventing delinquent debtors from obtaining new loans, loan guarantees, or loan insurance. Agencies can search the Debt Check database to determine if assistance applicants owe delinquent nontax debt to the federal government or owe delinquent child support. Rollout of Debt Check was completed in 2004, and six agencies are using the system.

We plan to perform a survey of the Debt Check program and related controls to identify risk areas that should be audited in more depth.

State Reciprocal Program Initiative

The Debt Collection Improvement Act of 1996 allows states to enter into reciprocal agreements with Treasury to collect unpaid state debt by offset of federal nontax payments, and the federal government to collect delinquent federal nontax debt by offset of state payments.

We plan to assess BFS' use of reciprocal agreements with states.

Managing Interchange Fees

In fiscal year 2012, Treasury, through FMS, collected approximately $10.7 billion in revenue through credit and debit cards and paid interchange fees of approximately $145.9 million. Interchange fees are payments that card-acquiring banks make to banks that issued the cards.

We plan to determine how BFS manages costs associated with interchange fees. As part of this audit, we plan to follow up on findings and recommendations from GAO's 2008 report, *Credit and Debit Cards: Federal Entities Are Taking Actions to Limit Their Interchange Fees, but Additional Revenue Collection Cost Savings May Exist* (GAO-08-558; May 15, 2008).

Selection and Monitoring of Financial Agents

We plan to assess Treasury's use of financial agency agreements to obtain services from financial institutions.

Projects under Consideration for Future Fiscal Years

Controls over the Check Forgery Insurance Fund

The Check Forgery Insurance Fund is a revolving fund administered by BFS to settle claims of non-receipt of Treasury checks. The fund's purpose is to ensure that the intended payees, whose checks were fraudulently negotiated, receive settlement in a timely manner. The OIG Office of Investigation is currently involved in a joint initiative with BFS in an effort to combat Treasury check fraud.

We plan to assess the controls over this fund.

Open Bank Accounts with Zero Balances

GAO reported in April 2012 that a BFS payment system, Automated Standard Application for Payments, held $126 million in grant accounts for which there had been no activity for 2 years or more. To help reduce unused funding, BFS issues dormant account reports to agencies who own the funds.

We plan to assess BFS' efforts to work with agencies to resolve dormant accounts with balances.

Delinquent Debt Referrals

Prompt referral of eligible debt to BFS by federal program agencies is critical to the success of collection efforts.

We plan to evaluate BFS' efforts to work with creditor federal agencies so that delinquent nontax debt is referred to BFS for collection in a timely manner.

Administrative Wage Garnishment

A collection tool available to BFS for nontax delinquent debt is Administrative Wage Garnishment (AWG), whereby a non-federal employer withholds a percentage of a delinquent employee's disposable income.

We plan to assess BFS' use of AWG.

Credit Bureau Reporting

Another collection tool available to BFS is reporting of nontax delinquent debt to credit bureaus.

We plan to assess BFS reporting of debt to credit bureaus.

Controls over the Treasury Check Information System

The Treasury Check Information System records and reconciles the issuance and payment of Treasury checks and allows end users to query Treasury's Payments, Claims and Enhanced Reconciliation system for claim status on Automated Clearing House payments. The system enables agencies to access all claim information in one system and is accessible through a standard web browser. The Treasury Check Information System was fully implemented in June 2006.

We plan to determine if the Treasury Check Information System is achieving its intended purposes.

Survey of Electronic Collection Methods

We plan to determine what actions BFS has taken to increase the use of electronic collections as a means to lower the cost of collections.

Survey of TreasuryDirect

We plan to perform a survey of the Treasury Direct program and related controls to identify risk areas that should be audited in more depth.

Collections and Cash Management Modernization Initiative

This initiative is a multi-year effort to simplify and modernize BFS and Treasury's collections and cash management programs. It involves re-architecting processes that have built up over decades. Its objectives are to (1) simplify collections and eliminate duplication; (2) provide federal agencies with detailed, centralized access to collection information; and (3) promote and expend the use of electronic collection of receipts.

We plan to assess the effectiveness of BFS' new cash management initiative.

Vendor Identity

We plan to assess BFS' controls to ensure vendors provide correct taxpayer information as required by the Debt Collection Improvement Act of 1996.

Survey of Treasury Securities Programs

BFS uses public auctions to sell marketable Treasury-issued securities to institutional and individual investors. In this regard, four types of securities are offered—bills, notes, bonds, and inflation-protected securities—264 public auctions were conducted in 2012. Treasury auctions occur on a set schedule and include three steps: (1) announcement of the auction, (2) bidding, and (3) issuance of the purchased securities. Our last examination of the auction process for Treasury securities was in 2000.

We plan to perform a survey of the auction process for Treasury securities and related controls to identify areas that, based on our assessment of risk, should be audited in more depth.

Survey of the Invoice Processing Platform

The Invoice Processing Platform is an Internet-based payment information portal provided by BFS for use, free of charge, to federal agencies and their vendors. It was established to improve the flow of information between federal agencies and suppliers by providing a centralized location to exchange electronic purchase orders, invoices, and related payment information. The system is available to all federal agencies and their suppliers.

We plan to gain an understanding of security measures and controls BFS uses for the portal to identify areas that, based on our assessment of risk, should be audited in more depth.

Lockbox Operations

BFS selects financial agents to provide lockbox remittance services for federal agencies. Lockbox processing was adopted to accelerate deposits to Treasury's General Account at the FRB of New York. Agencies instruct remitters to mail payments directly to a Treasury-designated lockbox bank. The bank processes remittance advices according to Treasury and agency instructions and transfers deposits daily to FRB of New York for credit to agency accounts. Treasury compensates lockbox banks for their services. For fiscal year 2012, total lockbox collections were approximately $348 billion, of which nontax collections were $28 billion.

We plan to assess BFS' oversight of lockbox services provided by financial agents.

Administrative Resource Center's Human Resource Function

We plan to evaluate the internal controls over the Administrative Resource Center's human resource service functions.

Debt Collection Improvement Act Exemptions

The Debt Collection Improvement Act of 1996 authorizes Treasury to grant federal agencies exemptions from transferring nontax delinquent debt to BFS. Treasury has granted exemptions to four agencies – the Department of Education, the Department of Health and Human Services, the Social Security Administration, and the Small Business Administration.

We plan to study the level of collection success and contributing factors/challenges of exempted agencies/programs compared to BFS' collection success on referred nontax delinquent debt.

Safety, Soundness, and Accessibility of Financial Services

Issue Area Discussion

One of Treasury's strategic goals is to repair and reform the financial system and support the recovery of the housing marker. Two of Treasury's strategies to reach that goal are to (1) continue efforts to implement comprehensive regulatory reform to increase stability and strengthen accountability in the financial system and (2) help prevent avoidable foreclosures and support the availability of affordable mortgage credit.

Dodd-Frank made sweeping changes to the U.S. financial regulatory framework, affecting all financial regulatory agencies, including OCC. It also established two offices within Treasury—the Office of Financial Research and the Federal Insurance Office.[3]

The Office of Financial Research, established by Title I of Dodd-Frank, is tasked with supporting the activities of the Financial Stability Oversight Council and its member agencies by performing activities such as collecting data on behalf of the council, providing data to the council and member agencies, standardizing the types and formats of data reported and collected, and performing essential long-term research. The Federal Insurance Office, established by Title V of Dodd-Frank, is tasked with addressing problems and concerns in the regulation of insurers that could contribute to a systemic crisis in the insurance industry or the U.S. financial system.

OCC is responsible for licensing, regulating, and supervising nearly 1,360 nationally chartered banks, 600 federal savings associations, and 50 federal branches or agencies of foreign banks. OCC-supervised banks hold over $10.1 trillion in total assets. OCC has over 3,800 employees. OCC has four strategic goals: (1) a safe and sound national banking and thrift system; (2) fair access to financial services and fair treatment of customers; (3) a flexible legal and regulatory framework that enables their respective industries to provide a full competitive array of financial services; and (4) an expert, highly motivated, and diverse workforce. OCC funds its operations largely through assessments levied on the financial institutions and from various licensing fees.

From September 2007 to June 30, 2013, 482 commercial banks and federal savings associations failed, resulting in an estimated $85.7 billion in losses to the Deposit Insurance Fund. Of these 479 failures, 130 were banks or federal savings associations regulated by OCC and/or the former OTS. Our office is mandated by Section 38(k) of the Federal Deposit Insurance Act to review and produce a written report on failures of OCC-regulated financial institutions that result in material losses to the fund. The law also requires that the report be completed within 6 months after it becomes apparent that a material loss has incurred. Dodd-Frank established the threshold loss amount triggering a material loss review to $150 million for 2012 and 2013, and $50 million in 2014 and thereafter, with a

---

[3] Dodd-Frank also established two other offices within Treasury—the Offices of Minority and Women Inclusion in Departmental Offices and OCC.

provision for increasing the threshold to $75 million under certain circumstances. To date, during the recent economic downturn, we have completed 54 material loss reviews.

Dodd-Frank also requires that for any failure of a OCC-regulated bank or thrift with a loss to the Deposit Insurance Fund under the threshold triggering a mandated material loss review, that we conduct a review that is limited to determining (1) the grounds identified by OCC for appointing FDIC as receiver, and (2) whether any unusual circumstances exist that might warrant an in-depth review of the loss.

In-Progress and Planned Fiscal Year 2014 Projects

Reviews of Failed OCC-Regulated Financial Institutions (Ongoing)

The purpose of a material loss review is to provide (1) an independent analysis of why the institution failed and resulted in a material loss; (2) evaluate the relevant regulator's supervision of the institution; and (3) as appropriate, make recommendations to prevent similar losses in the future. The reviews are performed by OIG staff. As of the date of this plan, we have one material loss review in progress: First National Bank, Edinburg, Texas.

For failed financial institutions with estimated losses under the material loss review threshold, we plan to determine (1) the grounds identified by OCC for appointing FDIC as receiver; and (2) whether any unusual circumstances exist that might warrant an in-depth review of the loss. To date, during the recent economic downturn, we have completed 65 limited reviews and are engaged in 1 other.

Transfer of OTS Functions (Ongoing)

Title III, Section 327 of Dodd-Frank requires that Treasury OIG, FDIC OIG, and FRB OIG jointly review the transfer of the functions, employees, funds, and property of OTS to FRB, FDIC, and OCC. In accordance with Title III, the transfer occurred in July 2011. Our first joint review, completed in March 2011, determined that the Joint Implementation Plan (Plan) for the transfer prepared by FRB, FDIC, OCC, and OTS conformed to relevant Title III provisions with one exception, which was corrected by an amendment to the Plan. After the initial joint review of the Plan, Section 327 requires that every 6 months we jointly provide a written report on the status of the implementation of the Plan. As of March 2013, we issued four reports under this requirement. In these reports, we concluded that FRB, FDIC, OCC, and OTS implemented the actions in the Plan that were necessary to transfer OTS functions, employees, and funds to FRB, FDIC, and OCC, and procedures and safeguards are in place as outlined in the Plan to ensure transferred employees are not unfairly disadvantaged. However, there are certain other items related to the Plan that are ongoing or are not yet required to be completed as provided in Title III.

In accordance with Section 327, we and the OIGs of FRB and FDIC will monitor and jointly report every 6 months on the implementation of the Plan until all aspects have been implemented. We expect that our final report for this mandate will be issued in March 2014.

Supervision of Bank Processes to Prevent, Detect, and Report Criminal Activity by Bank Employees (In-Progress)

We plan to (1) identify the extent and nature of criminal and other suspicious activity committed by bank and thrift employees reported to FinCEN under BSA through a review of Suspicious Activity Reports and related analytical studies; (2) identify OCC processes for pursuing enforcement action against current or former bank employees in which there is evidence of wrongdoing involving dishonesty or a breach of trust or money laundering; (3) identify OCC examination procedures to ensure national banks and federal savings associations have sufficient processes to prevent, detect, and report internal criminal activities; (4) determine if the procedures are applied effectively; and (5) determine if deficiencies identified during the examination process result in appropriate supervisory actions which are tracked and satisfactorily resolved.

Protection of Financial Services Sector Critical Infrastructure (In-Progress)

We plan to determine the effectiveness of Treasury's coordination efforts with private sector entities and other government entities to protect the banking and finance portions of the nation's critical infrastructure.

Lessons Learned from Bank Failures (In-Progress)

We plan to review completed material loss reviews and other reviews of Treasury-regulated failed financial institutions to (1) identify common themes related to the causes of failure and supervision of institutions, and (2) assess OCC's actions to strengthen the supervisory process in response to our audit recommendations as well as other initiatives by OCC.

Oversight of Amended Foreclosure-Related Consent Orders (In-Progress)

In April 2011, OCC issued formal enforcement actions against eight national bank mortgage servicers—Bank of America, N.A.; Citibank, N.A.; HSBC Bank USA, N.A.; JPMorgan Chase Bank, N.A.; MetLife Bank, N.A.; PNC Bank, N.A.; U.S. Bank National Association and U.S. Bank National Association ND; and Wells Fargo Bank, N.A. The former OTS issued formal enforcement actions, now administered by OCC, against four federal savings associations—Aurora Bank, FSB; Everbank and its thrift holding company, EverBank Financial Corp.; OneWest Bank, FSB and its holding company IMB HoldCo LLC; and, Sovereign Bank. The enforcement actions required the servicers to promptly correct deficiencies in residential mortgage loan servicing and foreclosure practices that examiners identified in reviews conducted during 2010. OCC's and OTS's enforcement actions also required each servicer to engage an independent firm to conduct a comprehensive review of foreclosure actions taken between January 1, 2009, and December 31, 2010, to identify and provide remediation to borrowers harmed.

In late 2012, OCC sought to end the independent foreclosure review process because the reviews were taking longer than anticipated and delaying compensation to the affected borrowers. In January 2013, OCC negotiated a change in terms of the consent orders with 10 of the 12 servicers. These new terms provided for immediate cessations of the independent review process, required servicers to make direct cash payments to potentially harmed borrowers, and required servicers to initiate a range of foreclosure relief actions over the course of the next 2 years. Two services did not agree to change their consent orders and were continuing the independent foreclosure review process.

We plan to report on the circumstances and processes used to determine that the foreclosure consent orders issued in April 2011 should be amended, including how the new settlement amounts were derived. We also plan to assess OCC's oversight of servicers' compliance with the amended consent orders to include oversight of (1) the servicers' categorization of the population of borrowers due payment; (2) the payment of funds from the Qualified Settlement Fund; and (3) the servicers' loss mitigation or other foreclosure prevention actions.

Review of the Establishment and Effectiveness of the Federal Insurance Office (In-Progress)

We plan to determine the status and effectiveness of Treasury's process to establish the Federal Insurance Office.

Supervision of Bank Trading Activities (In-Progress)

We plan to determine and assess OCC's process to supervise bank trading activities. We plan to initially focus on OCC's supervision of J.P. Morgan Chase, National Association.

Examination Coverage of Third-Party Service Providers (In-Progress)

We plan to assess OCC's examinations of third-party service providers used by OCC regulated banks.

Treasury's Controls over the Separation of Funds and Activities (In-Progress)

Consistent with a directive in House Report 112-550, we plan to assess the separation of funds and activities between mandatory-funded offices, such as the Office of Financial Research and the Office of Financial Stability, and discretionary-funded offices that carry out related work, such as Treasury's Office of Domestic Finance or Office of Economic Policy.

OCC's Property Leasing and Management Activities (In Progress)

We plan to (1) determine if OCC's real property leasing policies and procedures comply with applicable laws, rules, and regulations; (2) assess whether these policies and procedures are consistently followed; (3) review select OCC leases, to include its lease for new headquarters space, and assess whether the lease requirements were appropriate; and (4) review OCC's management and leasing activities related to the former OTS headquarters building.

OCC Supervision of U.S. Bank (In Progress)

We plan to assess OCC's supervision of U.S. Bank with respect to its mortgage lending activities.

Evaluation of Enforcement Actions against Institution-Affiliated Parties and Individuals (In Progress)

As part of a joint project with FDIC OIG and FRB OIG, we plan to study OCC's programs for pursuing enforcement actions against institution-affiliated parties and individuals associated with bank failures.

Office of Financial Research Performance Measures (In Progress)

We plan to assess the design and implementation of performance measures by the Office of Financial Research.

CIGFO Working Group Review

We plan to participate on at least one review as a member of a Council of Inspectors General on Financial Oversight (CIGFO) working group on Financial Stability Oversight Council processes.

Office of Financial Research Procurement Activities

We plan to determine if the Office of Financial Research's procurement process ensures that the Office of Financial Research effectively and efficiently acquires the goods and services needed to accomplish its mission and that procurements are made in compliance with applicable regulations.

OCC's Oversight of Servicers' Operational Improvements Required by the 2011 Foreclosure-Related Consent Orders

We plan to assess OCC's oversight of actions taken by servicers to address those articles of the 2011 foreclosure related consent orders designed to correct the unsafe and unsound operational practices.

Treasury's Implementation of PPD-21 and Executive Order Relating to Critical Infrastructure

We plan to assess Treasury's coordination efforts with private sector entities and other government entities to protect the banking and finance portions of the nation's critical infrastructure in accordance with Presidential Policy Directive-21, *Critical Infrastructure Security and Resilience* (February 2013), and E.O. 13636, *Improving Critical Infrastructure Cybersecurity*.

Supervision of Consumer Financial Protection and Compliance

We plan to assess OCC's (1) supervision over consumer protection and compliance at OCC-regulated financial institutions and (2) coordination with the Consumer Financial Protection Bureau and processing of consumer complaints involving national banks and federal savings associations with more than $10 billion.

Supervision of Large Institutions

We plan to assess OCC examinations of institutions with assets exceeding $100 billion.

Supervision of Student Loan Products

We plan to assess OCC's supervision of financial institutions' student loan lending activities.

Supervision of Small Banks

We plan to assess the safety and soundness challenges facing small banks and OCC's supervisory response to those challenges. Preliminarily, our focus will be on institutions with total assets of $250 million or less.

OCC Supervision of Payday Loans and Advanced Deposit Activities

We plan to assess OCC's supervision of payday loan and advanced deposit activities at financial institutions to ensure the use of safe and sound lending practices.

Supervision of Financial Institutions' Other Real Estate Owned Property

We plan to evaluate OCC's supervision of other real estate owned property in financial institutions. Our specific objectives are to determine if (1) guidance promoting effective assessment and control of other real estate owned property has been promulgated; (2) existing OCC monitoring, risk assessment, and examination procedures are sufficient to address other real estate owned property risk; (3) the procedures are applied effectively; and (4) deficiencies identified by OCC result in appropriate supervisory actions which are tracked and satisfactorily resolved.

Abandoned Foreclosures

We plan to assess OCC's oversight of banks' controls over risks associated with abandoned foreclosures.

Supervision of Foreign Country Risk

We plan to assess OCC's supervision of financial institutions' international exposures. Our specific objectives are to determine if (1) guidance promoting effective assessment and control of national banks' country risk has been promulgated; (2) existing OCC monitoring, risk assessment and examination procedures are sufficient to address country risk; (3) the procedures have been applied effectively; and (4) deficiencies identified during the examination process result in appropriate supervisory actions which are tracked and satisfactorily resolved.

Supervision of Federal Branches of Foreign Banks

We plan to assess OCC's supervision of foreign banking organizations operating in the U.S.

Examination Coverage of Identity Theft Risk at Financial Institutions

We plan to determine if OCC examinations of financial institutions are adequate to address privacy risks, including identity theft.

Legal Entity Identifier Implementation

We plan to assess progress made by the Office of Financial Research to implement a Legal Entity Identifier regime as a universal standard for identifying all parties to financial contracts.

Projects Under Consideration for Future Fiscal Years

Supervision of Incentive-Based Compensation Provisions of Dodd-Frank

Section 956 of Dodd-Frank requires financial institutions, with total consolidated assets of $1 billion or more, to disclose to the appropriate regulator the structures of all incentive-based compensation arrangements. The disclosure should allow the regulator to determine if the incentive-based compensation structure (1) provides executives, employees, directors, or principal shareholders with excessive compensation, fees or benefits or (2) could lead to material financial losses to the financial institution. Further, the law requires the federal regulators to jointly prescribe regulations or guidelines to provide for the disclosure of compensation arrangements and to prohibit any types of incentive-based payment arrangement that encourages inappropriate risks by the covered financial institution.

After the final rules are in place, we plan to assess OCC's supervision of incentive-based compensation structures in OCC-regulated financial institutions.

Identification and Reduction of Regulatory Burdens

E.O. 12866, *Regulatory Planning and Review*, issued in September 1993, established the regulatory planning process and guiding principles agencies must follow when developing regulations. The objectives of the E.O. are to (1) enhance planning and coordination with respect to both new and existing regulations, (2) reaffirm the primacy of federal agencies in the regulatory decision-making process (3) restore the integrity and legitimacy of regulatory oversight, and (4) make the process more accessible and open to the public.

To improve the transparency and accountability of agency rulemaking, the President issued E.O. 13563, *Improving Regulation and Regulatory Review*, in January 2011. The E.O. calls on agencies to promote public participation and an open exchange of information, and perspectives among State, local, and tribal officials, experts in relevant disciplines, affected stakeholders in the private sector, and the public as a whole. The E.O. also emphasizes the importance of retrospective analyses of existing rules, which states that that within 120 days, each agency shall develop a preliminary plan which should facilitate the periodic review of existing significant regulations and promote retrospective analysis of rules that may be outmoded, ineffective, insufficient, or excessively burdensome, and to modify, streamline, expand, or repeal them in accordance with what has been learned.

In May 2012, the President issued E.O. 13610, *Identifying and Reducing Regulatory Burdens*, to modernize the regulatory systems and reduce unjustified regulatory costs and burdens. The E.O. requires agencies to conduct retrospective analyses of current rules to examine whether they should be modernized or remained justified. The E.O. also states that agencies should promote public participation in retrospective review and report on the status of their retrospective efforts to Office of Information and Regulatory Affairs on a bi-annual basis.

We plan to assess Treasury's implementation of E.O. 13563 and E.O. 13610.

Development, Training, Rotation, and Performance Evaluations of OCC Examiners

We plan to assess OCC processes for developing, training, rotating, and evaluating the performance of bank examiners.

OCC Supervision of Insider Activities

We plan to assess OCC's supervision of insider activities at financial institutions.

OCC Supervision of Financial Institutions' Stress Testing Program

We plan to assess OCC's oversight of financial institutions' stress testing programs.

OCC Internal Bank Supervision Appeals Program

We plan to assess the OCC's Internal Bank Supervision Appeals.

Development and Communication of OCC Issuances and Comptrollers Handbook

We plan to assess OCC's processes to develop, update, communicate, and promote the consistent use of OCC issuances (bulletins, alerts) and the Comptrollers Handbook.

Supervision of Real Estate Appraisal Activities

We plan to assess OCC's supervision of financial institutions' real estate appraisal and evaluation policies and procedures.

OCC's Licensing and Charter Approval Process

We plan to assess the OCC's licensing and charter conversion process for financial institutions.

Safeguards Over Financial Institutions' Sensitive Information

We plan to determine if OCC examiners adhere to applicable laws, regulations, and policies and procedures for safeguarding the privacy and confidentiality of sensitive information financial institutions provide to OCC during the examination process.

Supervision of Nonbanking Activities of Financial Institutions

We plan to assess OCC supervision of nonbanking activities of regulated financial institutions and their affiliates.

OCC's Alternatives to the Use of Credit Ratings

Section 939A of Dodd-Frank contains two directives to federal agencies including the OCC. First, Section 939A directs all federal agencies to review, no later than 1 year after enactment, any regulation that requires the use of an assessment of creditworthiness of a security or money market instrument and any references to, or requirements in, such regulations regarding credit ratings. Second, the agencies are required to remove any references to, or requirements of reliance on, credit ratings and substitute such standard of creditworthiness as each agency determines is appropriate. The statute further provides that the agencies shall seek to establish, to the extent feasible, uniform standards of creditworthiness, taking into account the entities the agencies regulate and the purposes for which those entities would rely on such standards.

We plan to assess OCC's implementation of guidance on alternatives to the use of credit ratings by financial institutions to determine the creditworthiness of securities and money market instruments.

Supervisory Use of Individual Minimum Capital Requirements

We plan to assess how OCC applies capital restrictions and risk-weighting to institutions they supervise to include (1) OCC's use of individual minimum capital requirements as an enforcement action, (2) the criteria used to calculate the capital requirement, and (3) how the minimum capital requirements are enforced.

Supervision of Large Banks' Internal Audit Function

We plan to assess the effectiveness and adequacy of OCC's supervision of the overall audit function of banks with assets exceeding $100 billion.

OCC Oversight of Credit Risk Retention

We plan to assess OCC's oversight of financial institutions credit-risk retention once the final rules are issued.

OCC Enforcement Practices

We plan to assess OCC's enforcement practices, including (1) the factors used to determine the use of formal and informal enforcement actions, (2) the timeliness of enforcement actions, (3) controls to ensure consistency in the use of enforcement actions, and (4) the manner in which OCC ensures compliance with enforcement actions.

Federal Insurance Office Performance Measures

We plan to assess the design and implementation of performance measures by the Federal Insurance Office.

OCC's Participation in the Shared National Credit Program

The Shared National Credit Program was formed in 1977 to provide an efficient and consistent review and classification of large syndicated loans. The program was established by OCC, FDIC, and FRB. The program covers any loan or loan commitment of at least $20 million and shared by three or more supervised institutions. The agencies' review is conducted annually. We plan to evaluate OCC's participation in the Shared National Credit Program. Our specific objectives are to (1) identify the guidance promoting effective review of shared national credits; (2) determine if existing monitoring, risk assessments and examination procedures are sufficient to address risk to the banking industry by shared national credits; (3) determine if the procedures are applied effectively; and (4) determine if deficiencies identified during the examination process resulted in appropriate supervisory actions which are tracked and satisfactorily resolved.

Supervision of Interest Rate Risk

We plan to assess OCC's examination coverage related to financial institutions' risk management over interest rate risk.

Commercial Real Estate Concentrations

We plan to determine the risks associated with financial institutions having high commercial real estate concentrations and related OCC supervisory approaches.

Revenue Collection and Industry Regulation

Issue Area Discussion

TTB collects federal excise taxes on tobacco products, alcohol, and firearms and ammunition. The bureau also ensures compliance with tobacco and alcohol permitting requirements as well as ensures alcohol products are properly labeled, advertised, and marketed. In addition, the bureau ensures fair trade practices and facilitates the international trade of alcohol beverage products. TTB administers and enforces the (1) Internal Revenue Code pertaining to the excise taxation and authorized operations of alcohol and tobacco producers and related industries,;(2) Federal Alcohol Administration Act; (3) Alcohol Beverage Labeling Act; and (4) Webb-Kenyon Act, which prohibits the shipment of alcohol beverages into a state in violation of the state's laws. The bureau is headquartered in Washington, D.C., and maintains its tax and permit processing center at the National Revenue Center, in Cincinnati, Ohio. TTB's Tax Audit Division has six district field office locations as does its Trade Investigations Division. TTB also has alcohol and tobacco laboratories in Maryland and California.

During fiscal year 2012, TTB collected $23.4 billion in excise taxes and other revenue from about 8,500 excise taxpayers. Congress authorized TTB funding in 2010 and 2012 to establish a criminal enforcement program to address tobacco smuggling and other diversion activity. With a $2 million annual appropriation, TTB entered into an agreement with IRS Criminal Investigation (IRS CI) for criminal investigative services to enforce its criminal jurisdiction. In its 2 years of operation, TTB opened a total of 48 cases with an estimated tax liability of $340 million.

In fiscal year 2011, TTB launched two e-Gov systems—Permits Online and Formulas Online—to allow customers to access TTB through the Web. In FY 2012, TTB completed its implementation of Permits Online with a third system release that enabled electronic filing for its remaining high-volume permit types: breweries, distilled spirits plants, alcohol fuel plants, tobacco manufacturers and processors, and firearms manufacturers. The overall adoption rate for Permits Online was 62 percent. TTB received 49 percent of its alcohol beverage formula submissions electronically through Formulas Online. TTB monitored compliance with permitting requirements through data analysis and investigative techniques. TTB intelligence analysts identified 13 percent of active tobacco importers illegally imported products, and cease and desist letters were sent to these importers.

The bureau also reviews labels and formulas for domestic and imported beverage alcohol products and maintains public access to approved Certificates of Label Approval (COLA), which are required for every alcoholic beverage. Nearly 140,000 (91 percent) of the COLAs received by TTB in FY 2012 were submitted online. TTB monitors labeling compliance through the Alcohol Beverage Sampling Program and tests samples of wine, distilled spirits, and malt beverages for content in its in-house laboratories.

In addition to its tax and regulatory functions, TTB helps facilitate global alcohol trade, including exports of wine and spirits that most recently totaled approximately $3 billion. Through formal international agreements, TTB engaged regulators from Canada, China, the European Union, France, Italy, Mexico, and the World Wine Trade Group.

The Secretary of the Treasury has authority for Customs revenue functions, and this authority is delegated to the Office of Tax Policy. The Homeland Security Act of 2002 transferred the legacy U.S. Customs Service from Treasury to the Department of Homeland Security in March 2003, where it became Customs and Border Protection. However, as provided by the act, Treasury retained sole authority to approve any regulations concerning import quotas or trade bans, user fees, marking, labeling, copyright and trademark enforcement, and the completion of entry or substance of entry summary, including duty assignment and collection, classification, valuation, application of the U.S. Harmonized Tariff Schedules, eligibility or requirements for preferential trade programs, and the establishment of related recordkeeping requirements. Treasury also reviews Customs and Border Protection rulings involving these topics if they constitute a change in practice.

Potential Integrity Risks

The major integrity risks for TTB involve not collecting all revenue rightfully due and having alcohol products in the marketplace that are improperly labeled. The failure by industry members to pay all taxes due, either intentionally or otherwise, coupled with the risk that the TTB tax verification and audit program may not detect these underpayments, or that industry members could attempt to corrupt government officials through bribery or other means, could seriously undermine TTB's tax collection activity. Similarly, fraudulent manufacturers or distributors could attempt to place untaxed, unsafe, or deceptively advertised products into the marketplace.

Notwithstanding the attractiveness of evading alcohol taxes through product diversion and smuggling, the passage of the Children's Health Insurance Program Reauthorization Act of 2009 (CHIPRA) provided added incentive to evade tobacco taxes. Specifically, CHIPRA increased the federal excise tax on all tobacco products, including an increase of more than 150 percent on cigarettes. CHIPRA required Treasury to conduct a study concerning the magnitude of illicit tobacco trade in the U.S. The study found that accurately measuring the amount of federal tax receipts lost from tobacco diversion and smuggling was difficult due to its inherently clandestine nature, but that significant losses could be occurring. In its 2012 annual report, TTB stated that tax receipts were diminished by as much as $1.5 billion annually for the years 2005 to 2007 due to smuggling and other criminal diversion activity. Considering the current rate and other factors remaining constant, TTB stated the potential federal revenue losses from cigarette diversion could be $5 billion annually. The study also identified several weaknesses in the control of tobacco products which can directly affect tax collection. While manufacturers and importers of tobacco products and processed tobacco must have permits to operate and are subject to recordkeeping requirements, the same is not true of tobacco brokers, wholesalers, and retailers of tobacco products. Also, access to machinery used to manufacture cigarettes is unrestricted and may be used to violate the tax code.

Enacted in July 2012, the Moving Ahead for Progress in the 21st Century Act (MAP-21) addressed the legal status of retailers that provide cigarette making equipment on their premises for use by customers to manufacture cigarettes. Under MAP-21, any person who, for commercial purposes, makes available for consumer use a machine capable of making tobacco products (including cigarettes), is a manufacturer of tobacco products under the Internal Revenue Code. As manufacturers of tobacco products, these establishments fall under the jurisdiction of TTB. Manufacturers of tobacco products, however small, must comply with all applicable statutory and regulatory requirements.

Internet sales remain an area of concern for TTB's revenue collection responsibilities, as the bureau must coordinate with the U.S. Postal Service and ground carriers for enforcement assistance.

In-Progress and Planned Fiscal Year 2014 Projects

Tax Receipts Lost Due to Illicit Trade (In-Progress)

Section 703 of CHIPRA directed the Secretary of the Treasury to conduct a study concerning the magnitude of illicit tobacco trade in the U.S. and to submit to Congress a report with recommendations for the most effective steps to reduce illicit tobacco trade. The resulting Treasury study used a tax gap analysis to determine the magnitude of tax receipts lost and included three recommendations to address this issue.

We plan to assess actions taken by TTB in response to the Treasury study or other actions taken to mitigate tax losses. We also plan to assess whether a similar tax gap analysis should be used to identify tax receipts lost due to illicit alcohol trade.

TTB's Use of Collection Procedures and Offers in Compromise to Collect Revenue (In-Progress)

TTB is responsible for collection efforts on delinquent taxpayer accounts including the assessment of interest and penalties on late or unfiled tax returns as well as late or underpayments of taxes due. TTB uses several collection tools including the levy of bank accounts, liens placed on taxpayer property, and forfeiture of bond proceeds to resolve delinquent tax cases. TTB also uses offers in compromise to resolve outstanding taxes due in lieu of civil or criminal proceedings.

We plan to assess TTB's collection procedures for delinquent accounts, including write-offs of delinquent debts that are no longer collectable. We also plan to assess TTB's use of offers in compromise in its collection activities.

TTB Controls Over the Alcohol and Tobacco Permit Program

We plan to assess TTB's controls over issuance of alcohol and tobacco permits and efforts to identify and obtain permits from new industry members added to TTB's regulatory responsibilities under CHIPRA, and MAP-21. As part of this work, we plan to assess TTB's Permits Online program.

TTB's Oversight of Newly Defined Manufacturers of Tobacco Products Under MAP-21

We plan to assess TTB's efforts in identifying new tobacco product manufacturers, enforcing the new regulatory requirements, and monitoring the labeling of tobacco used in the on-site manufacturing of tobacco products.

TTB Designation of American Viticultural Areas

An American Viticultural Area is a designated wine-grape-growing region with features that affect the growing conditions of the area (climate, soil, elevation, physical features) and that distinguish it from surrounding areas.

We plan to assess the controls in place over TTB's program to designate American Viticultural Areas.

Projects Under Consideration for Future Fiscal Years

TTB's Tax Verification Process

TTB's tax verification process incorporates a strategic risk-based approach to conduct targeted compliance audits and investigations of industry members. In FY 2012, TTB increased automation for its investigative targeting models. TTB used data for enforcement actions to identify industry members and others that could be involved in diversion and tax fraud. We plan to assess TTB's excise tax verification process.

TTB's Efforts to Ensure the Accurate Collection of Federal Excise Taxes on Imports

We plan to assess TTB's efforts to identify federal excise taxes due on undeclared and misclassified alcohol and tobacco product imports and TTB's coordination with the Customs and Border Patrol to ensure all federal excise taxes due are paid by importers.

Effect of CHIPRA on Tax Paid Removals of Tobacco Products

Federal excise taxes are imposed on tobacco products when they are removed for sale from manufacturers or when they are imported into the U.S. In 2009, CHIPRA significantly increased the tax rates on all tobacco products. The tax rates for pipe tobacco and roll-your-own tobacco, previously taxed at similar rates, were increased to $2.83 per pound and $24.78 per pound, respectively. TTB's analysis of the tobacco industry identified a dramatic shift in the reported removals of roll-your-own tobacco in favor of lower taxed pipe tobacco. TTB also identified an immediate shift in the cigar market from small cigars to lower taxed large cigars. Revenue loss estimates associated with these transitions may exceed $1 billion. A 2012 study by GAO confirmed TTB's revenue loss estimates and concluded that TTB will face significant challenges ensuring the proper amounts of tax are paid. GAO recommended Congress consider equalizing tax rates and working with Treasury to consider other options to reduce tax avoidance.

We plan to assess TTB's efforts to ensure all appropriate taxes are paid, and determine the impact of CHIPRA tax increases on reported removals of other products such as large and small cigars that are subject to different tax rates.

TTB Alcohol and Tobacco Laboratory Services

We plan to review TTB's alcohol and tobacco laboratories service to TTB program units. As part of the audit, we plan to assess TTB's efforts to ensure the safety of imported beverage products through pre-import activities, post-market sampling, and laboratory analysis.

TTB Reviews of Manufacturer Nonbeverage Drawback Claims

When a manufacturer uses alcohol to produce a food, flavor, medicine, or perfume that is approved by TTB's Nonbeverage Products Laboratory as unfit for beverage purposes, the manufacturer can claim a return, or drawback, on most of the distilled spirits excise tax paid. In fiscal year 2012, approved nonbeverage drawback claims totaled $307 million.

We plan to assess TTB's controls over nonbeverage product manufacturer claims.

TTB's Regulatory Oversight of Manufacturers of Processed Tobacco

CHIPRA established TTB's responsibility for oversight of manufacturers of processed tobacco. These manufacturers receive tobacco plants from growers, remove the stems, and cut the tobacco leaves. The processed tobacco is used by manufacturers that produce tobacco products such as cigarettes and cigars. Both domestically grown and imported processed tobacco is generally not subject to federal excise tax until manufactured into tobacco products and removed for consumption in the U.S. In 2010, the market for processed tobacco was approximately 1.1 billion pounds. Manufacturers of processed tobacco can legally sell processed tobacco to product manufacturers, other businesses that further process the tobacco, or tobacco brokers, many of whom are not licensed to operate by TTB. Manufacturers of processed tobacco are required to report to TTB sales of processed tobacco to businesses without TTB permits. Because of regulatory restrictions, TTB cannot always follow the processed tobacco through the industry pipeline to determine what products the processed tobacco was manufactured into and if federal excise taxes were paid.

We plan to (1) determine what actions TTB has taken to regulate manufacturers of processed tobacco, (2) determine how TTB has used its authority to detect and prevent processed tobacco from entering the illicit market, and (3) identify regulatory-related issues impacting TTB's ability to prevent illicit tobacco trade related to processed tobacco.

TTB Use of Collateral to Protect Revenue

TTB protects excise tax revenue by mandating that taxpayers pledge collateral—such as a bond, note, or securities—to offset tax liability if payments are not made.

We plan to determine if TTB is ensuring that taxpayers maintain adequate collateral to protect tax revenue.

Coordinating Participation in the International Trade Data System Project

The Security and Accountability for Every Port Act (SAFE Port Act) formally established the International Trade Data System, a system for processing imports and exports. The system is operated by Customs and Border Protection in collaboration with 43 agencies. The act gave the Secretary of the Treasury responsibility for coordinating interagency participation in the system. One of its features allows TTB to review data on importations of alcohol and tobacco through the Customs and Border Protection automated commercial environment portal. TTB is also to provide

Customs and Border Protection access to its database of approved alcohol labels, which will allow Customs inspectors to compare the approved labels with the actual labels on the imported products.

We plan to determine if Treasury is fulfilling its responsibility under the SAFE Port Act. We also plan to determine if the information sharing between TTB and Customs has proved beneficial in ensuring only approved products are imported.

Impact of National Revenue Center Tax Services Branch Reorganization

The Tax Services Branch of TTB's National Revenue Center processes taxpayer returns and payments, evaluates claims for reimbursement, and performs collections activity on delinquent taxpayer accounts. In September 2012, Tax Services was the subject of a reorganization due to TTB's declining budgetary authority, reduced staffing levels, and increased workload. As part of the reorganization, the National Revenue Center rolled out an in-house developed document tracking system. TracDoc was designed to facilitate document and case management and the efficient distribution of the Tax Services workload to ensure the most effective use of resources.

We plan to assess the Tax Services reorganization.

TTB Online Certification of Label Approval and Formulas Online

The purpose of the COLA program is to protect the public from false or misleading labels on alcohol beverage products. The program requires importers and bottlers of alcohol beverages to obtain a certificate of label approval or certificate of exemption prior to placing the beverages into interstate commerce. In 2003, TTB initiated COLA Online which allows users to electronically file COLA applications. In FY 2012, approximately 91 percent of the COLA applications were submitted online exceeding TTB's target goal of 88 percent.

COLA Online was enhanced in January 2011 with the first deployment of Formulas Online which enabled alcohol beverage producers and importers to electronically file their formulae with TTB for approval. Formulas Online is a Web-based system that allows external users to draft, submit, and track formula applications for alcohol beverage products and for flavors that contain alcohol.

We plan to determine if COLA Online, including the Formulas Online application, is operating as intended, including whether any user problems have been identified and, if so, corrected.

TTB Controls over Cover-Over Payments

Taxes collected on rum produced in Puerto Rico or the U.S. Virgin Islands and transported to the U.S. are "covered over" or transferred to the territory where the rum is produced. Taxes collected on rum imported into the U.S. from foreign countries are also covered over to the two territories; the payments are split between Puerto Rico and the U.S. Virgin Islands. In fiscal year 2012, TTB processed cover over payments totaling $386 million to the treasuries of Puerto Rico and the U.S. Virgin Islands.

We plan to determine if TTB's controls ensure that cover-over reimbursements are made for the correct amounts and in a timely manner.

Bill and Coin Manufacturing, Marketing, and Distribution Operations

Issue Area Discussion

BEP produces U.S. currency and other security documents issued by the federal government. BEP also processes claims for the redemption of mutilated paper currency and provides technical assistance and advice to other federal agencies on the design and production of documents requiring counterfeit deterrence. BEP has production facilities in Washington, D.C., and Fort Worth, Texas.

In fiscal year 2012, BEP delivered 8.4 billion Federal Reserve notes to FRB compared to the 5.8 billion delivered in fiscal year 2011. BEP planned delivery of the redesigned NexGen $100 notes to FRB in late 2010 for the anticipated public release in February 2011. However, problems in the production process of these notes delayed the 2011 release date. In April 2013, the FRB announced a new release date of October 2013 for the NexGen $100 note.

The Mint's principal mission is to produce the nation's circulation coinage for trade and commerce. The Mint also produces commemorative and investment products for collectors and investors. In addition to its headquarters in Washington, D.C., the Mint has four production facilities located in Philadelphia, West Point, Denver, and San Francisco. It also maintains the U.S. bullion depository at Fort Knox.

In fiscal year 2012, the Mint manufactured 9.1 billion coins for the Federal Reserve which is an increase of 37 percent compared to the 7.4 billion produced in fiscal year 2011. The Mint expects circulating coin production volumes in 2014 to increase to 9.5 billion, about a 13 percent increase over fiscal year 2013 projections of 8.4 billion. In December 2011, Treasury suspended the circulating dollar coin production as part of the Campaign to Cut Waste and in recognition of the large holdings of dollar coins at the Federal Reserve. The suspension resulted in increases to the demand of other coins but decreases to the Mint's circulating revenue by about 37 percent and seignorage by 70 percent.

In fiscal year 1996, the Mint Public Enterprise Fund was created to enable the Mint to operate as a revolving fund. All receipts deposited into the fund are available for Mint operations and the cost of safeguarding government assets in the Mint's custody, without fiscal year limitations. Even though the Mint is not dependent on appropriated funds, its spending authority is approved by Congress each fiscal year. The Secretary of the Treasury must annually determine the amount of excess in the fund that is not needed for Mint operations for transfer to the Treasury General Fund. For fiscal year 2012, the Mint transferred $77 million to the Treasury General Fund. This amount is higher than 2011 but significantly lower than years past—transferred amounts were $388 million in fiscal year 2010 and $475 million in fiscal year 2009. The Mint reported in its fiscal year 2012 annual report that it is holding cash in reserve for future potential impacts to its circulating program from the continued penny and nickel losses, and the loss in revenue from the suspension of the $1 coin production.

Potential Weaknesses

Because their operations are financed through revolving funds, BEP and the Mint are subject to fewer congressional controls than appropriated agencies. The Mint also has greater flexibility in conducting its procurement activities, because the Mint is exempt from the Federal Acquisition Regulation. Prudent use by the Mint of its fund authority flexibilities is necessary to ensure a maximum return to the Treasury General Fund.

Continuing Issue with BEP Concerning Currency Products that Cannot Be Readily Recognized by Blind and Visually Impaired Individuals

In 2006, a federal judge ruled that the Department's failure to design, produce, and issue paper currency that is readily distinguishable to blind and visually impaired individuals violated federal law. Two years later, a federal appeals court ruled that the U.S. discriminates against blind and visually impaired individuals by producing currency that they cannot recognize without the assistance of others. In conjunction with this decision and in consultation with BEP and Department of Justice attorneys, a federal judge ruled that the next generation of $5, $10, $20, and $50 notes must be manufactured so that blind and visually impaired individuals can tell them apart. This ruling did not affect the design of the new $100 note, but future designs must ensure that all denominations, except for the $1 note, be distinguishable from other notes.

Potential Integrity Risks

Past audits have noted various weaknesses in BEP's physical security. As noted in the most recent report, *Bill and Coin Manufacturing: Improved Security Over the NexGen $100 Notes Is Necessary,* (OIG-11-068; May 13, 2011), management took corrective action on a serious weakness found by our auditors in the security over NexGen $100 finished notes and work-in-process sheets at both BEP's Eastern Currency Facility and Western Currency Facility. Previously in fiscal year 2008, as discussed in *Bill and Coin Manufacturing: BEP Needs to Enforce and Strengthen Controls at Its Eastern Currency Facility to Prevent and Detect Employee Theft,* (OIG-08-036; June 12, 2008), following a theft at the Eastern Currency Facility we found that BEP did not ensure that production supervisors enforced, and employees adhered to, existing internal controls. Additionally, no policies and procedures were in place to investigate production discrepancies. Issues with BEP's information security were also noted in a recent report, *BEP's Network and Systems Security Was Found to Be Insufficient,* (OIG-11-112; Sep. 30, 2011). We found BEP did not establish sufficient protection for its network and systems to protect against insider threats and noted critical vulnerabilities caused by a number of missing security patches.

In-Progress and Planned Fiscal Year 2014 Projects

BEP's Project Management of the Enterprise Network System (In-Progress)

BEP's Enterprise Network System (BEN) project is intended to simplify and standardize procedures, increase efficiency, and eliminate unnecessary processes at BEP to increase product quality, reduce spoilage, and improve accountability.

We plan to determine if (1) the BEN project business case is based on appropriate and supportable assumptions and cost/benefit estimates; (2) sound project management principles are followed in carrying out BEN; and (3) federal regulations and guidance, Treasury directives, and BEP policies and procedures are followed in conjunction with the project.

Physical Security at Mint Facilities (In-Progress)

Because Mint facilities house precious metals (gold, silver and platinum), investment grade bullion products, and billions of circulating coins, it is imperative that the products stored are protected from theft and other unauthorized access.

We plan to (1) assess the Mint's physical security policies and procedures and (2) determine if the facilities' physical security conforms to those policies and procedures.

Mint Controls Over the Sales of Limited-Production, Investment-Grade Products (In-Progress)

In addition to manufacturing circulating coins and numismatic products made available to the public, the Mint also sells precious metal (gold, silver and platinum) investment grade bullion coins to pre-qualified authorized purchasers for resale to the public.

We plan to determine if the Mint has adequate controls to ensure the broadest and most fair access to its products.

Mint's Pitney Bowes Contract (In-Progress)

The Mint uses Pitney Bowes to perform order fulfillment precious metal (gold, silver and platinum) investment grade bullion and commemorative products at a non-Mint location.

We plan to assess the contractor's facility operations.

BEP's Production Process for the NexGen $100 Notes (In-Progress)

In response to significant problems encountered by BEP in the production process and at the request of the Department, we plan to assess BEP's (1) planning and implementation of the NexGen $100 Notes production process and the events that lead to the problems in the production process; (2) on-going physical security over the notes that have been produced; (3) plans for the disposition of those notes; and (4) actions, taken and planned, to address the production problems. In May 2011, we issued the first report on our observations regarding physical security over the NexGen $100 notes (*Bill Manufacturing: Improved Security Over the NexGen $100 Notes Is Necessary*, OIG-11-068). In January 2012, we issued a second report detailing findings and recommendations regarding BEP's project management (*Bill Manufacturing: Improved Planning and Production Oversight Over the NexGen $100 Note Is Critical*, OIG-12-038). We plan to issue a third report during fiscal year 2014 related to physical security as a follow-up to our first report.

BEP and Mint Human Resources Practices

We plan to determine if the BEP and the Mint conducts the human resources activities with respect to hiring senior level positions in accordance with federal and Treasury requirements and BEP and Mint policies and procedures.

BEP Currency Project to Accommodate the Blind and Visually Impaired

We plan to determine if BEP's plan to create meaningful access to U.S. currency for blind and visually impaired individuals (1) meets the terms mandated by a court order issued in 2008 and the needs of users and (2) utilized proper cost/benefit analysis.

BEP and Mint Forecasting: Impact of Electronic Payments

We plan to assess efforts to strategically analyzes currency and coin needs based on consumer usage preferences, and to determine how the BEP and Mint incorporate changing payment trends (cash vs. electronic payments) into their long-range planning activities.

Mint Production Costs Studies

The Mint's costs (e.g., cost of the metal, fabrication, and other direct and indirect expenses) to produce pennies and nickels have more than double the face value of the coins produced since fiscal year 2006. This is the seventh straight year where production costs for these coins exceeded their face values.

We plan to assess whether studies the Mint has undertaken comply with the intent of the Coin Modernization, Oversight, and Continuity Act of 2010 to advise Congress of the potential for reducing production costs of circulating coins.

BEP's Facilities Studies and Continuity of Operations Planning

In early 2012, BEP completed a study of the infrastructure and repairs needs of the Eastern Currency Facility, which was built in the early 1900's. Within the next several years, BEP plans to coordinate with the Federal Reserve to decide whether to upgrade its current facility and/or procure a new facility.

We plan to determine if BEP's facilities study and resulting investment decisions are based on appropriate and supportable assumptions and cost/benefit estimates. We also plan to determine if BEP comprehensively developed and tested continuity of operations plans for currency production should a major disruption occur at one or both its production facilities.

Projects under Consideration for Future Fiscal Years

Mint Commemorative Coin Programs

Congress authorizes commemorative coins that celebrate and honor American people, places, events, and institutions. Although these coins are legal tender, they are not intended for general circulation. The Mint produces limited quantities of commemorative coins and makes them available for a short period of time.

We plan to assess the Mint's management of the commemorative coin programs and related surcharges.

BEP and Mint Employee Safety

We plan to assess BEP and Mint's efforts to ensure safe working conditions in the production facilities. Separate audits are planned of the facilities.

BEP's Capital Investment Program

We plan to determine if BEP's capital investment program ensures that all capital needs are identified and that sufficient funds are allocated and set aside to meet current and future capital needs.

Mint Order Fulfillment

We plan to determine if the Mint implemented adequate controls for its customer service and order fulfillment process to ensure adequate customer service is provided and costs are controlled.

America the Beautiful Silver Coin Program

Public Law 110-456 enacted the America the Beautiful Quarters program which also allows the Mint to manufacture silver bullion quarters coins with the same design as the circulating coins. The act requires that the bullion coins be available for sale no sooner than the first day of the calendar year in which the corresponding circulating quarter coin is issued and only during the year in which the circulating quarter coin is issued.

We plan to determine if the Mint is effectively managing the America the Beautiful bullion coin program and ensuring compliance with Public Law 110-456, as it relates to the sales period for each coin.

Mint Sales General and Administrative Expense Allocation

In 2011, the Mint reported a change to its sales, general, and administrative expenses allocation methodology intended to more accurately represent costs incurred for each coin denomination.

We plan to determine if the Mint's recent changes to the allocation of selling, general, and administrative expenses are consistent with managerial cost accounting principles.

Domestic and International Assistance Programs

Issue Area Discussion

Treasury plays an important role in a number of domestic and international assistance programs that have a significant impact on the economy. Domestic programs range from those that enhance the availability of financial education, credit, investment capital, and financial services to communities around the U.S., to programs that assist in coping with the effects of the current economic conditions. Treasury's role in these areas expanded under HERA, the Emergency Economic Stabilization Act of 2008 (which created TARP), the Recovery Act, Dodd-Frank, and the Small Business Jobs Act of 2010.

International programs address the role of international financial institutions and promote economic stability and growth in other countries.

HERA

The purpose of the act is to address problems and concerns in the mortgage and banking industries. Among other things, the act established the Federal Housing Finance Agency (FHFA) as an independent agency to oversee Federal National Mortgage Association (Fannie Mae) and Federal Home Loan Mortgage Corporation (Freddie Mac), and the Federal Home Loan Banks. The act also established the Federal Housing Finance Oversight Board to advise the agency with respect to overall strategies and policies in carrying out its responsibilities. The Secretary of the Treasury is a member of this board. It also assigned Treasury new authorities and responsibilities. Although certain Treasury purchase authorities under HERA expired in December 2009, Treasury maintains a sizeable investment in the Fannie Mae and Freddie Mac.

- **Government Sponsored Enterprises** In connection with the increased federal regulatory oversight of Fannie Mae, Freddie Mac, and the Federal Home Loan Banks, the act increased Treasury's authority over existing lines of credit to the entities that gave the Secretary of the Treasury standby, unlimited authority to buy stock or debt in them. To do so, the Secretary made an emergency determination required by HERA that use of the authority was necessary to stabilize markets, prevent disruptions in mortgage availability, and protect the taxpayer. Through Senior Preferred Stock Purchase Agreements, Treasury has provided financial support to Fannie Mae and Freddie Mac after any quarter that the entities report net worth deficiencies. In exchange, the liquidation preference of Treasury-owned senior preferred stock is increased. In August 2012, Treasury announced a set of modifications to the Senior Preferred Stock Purchase Agreements to facilitate the wind down of Fannie Mae and Freddie Mac and support the continued flow of mortgage credit toward a responsible transition to a reformed housing finance market. The modified agreements required an accelerated reduction of Fannie Mae and Freddie Mac's investment portfolios, to 15 percent annually from 10 percent annually. As a result of this change, the GSEs' investment portfolios are to be reduced to the $250 billion target set in the previous agreements 4 years earlier than previously scheduled. The modified agreements also require that on an annual basis, each GSE will submit a plan to Treasury on its strategy to reduce financial and operational risk, as well as an assessment of their performance relative to their prior year's plan Furthermore, the modified agreements replaced the 10 percent dividend payments made to Treasury on its preferred stock investments in Fannie Mae and Freddie Mac with a quarterly sweep of the net worth amount less a capital reserve amount which begins at $3 billion and reduces annual by an equal amount until it reaches zero beginning January 1, 2018. As of June 30, 2013, Treasury reported investments totaling $187 billion in senior preferred stock of the two GSEs.

- **HFA Initiative** In addition, Treasury implemented the Housing Finance Agency (HFA) Initiative with two programs to support state and local HFAs. Through those programs, Treasury purchased securities from Fannie Mae and Freddie Mac backed by state and local HFA bonds (New Issue Bond Program) and participation interests in liquidity facilities provided to the HFAs by Fannie Mae and Freddie Mac (Temporary Credit and Liquidity Program). As of June 30, 2013, Treasury owns 10.9 billion of Fannie Mae and Freddie Mac securities supporting the New Issue Bond Program and $3.3 billion participation interest in the Temporary Credit and Liquidity Program.

- **Capital Magnet Fund** The act also authorized a new program for CDFI Fund to administer— the Capital Magnet Fund (CMF). It is intended to create a new source of grants for both rental and for-sale housing, as well as for community and economic development. The program is supposed to increase the flow of capital to organizations that will engage in housing-related investments. The CMF is a competitive grant program expected to attract private capital. There are two types of eligible grantees under the fund: (1) CDFIs that have been certified by CDFI Fund, and (2) nonprofit organizations having as one of their principal purposes the development or management of affordable housing. The eligible grant activities and entities eligible to receive grants through the CMF represent a significant expansion for CDFI Fund's core programs. The CMF was funded $80 million through appropriation in fiscal year 2010 for its inaugural award round. Since then, CDFI Fund has not requested to fund the CMF. Under HERA, it was intended that the CMF would be financed through appropriation and transfers from Fannie Mae and Freddie which has not occurred due to the financial condition of the two entities.

Recovery Act

The purpose of the Recovery Act was to provide relief during the current economic downturn by expanding tax, bond, and cash assistance to segments of the economy most affected. Treasury is responsible for overseeing an estimated $150 billion provided through tax relief and Recovery Act funding. An estimated $24 billion in Recovery Act Funds, administered by Departmental Offices through two tax credit exchange programs, provide payments in lieu of tax credits for specified energy properties and payments to the states in lieu of tax credits for rehabilitation and development of low-income housing projects.

Other Domestic Assistance

Treasury provides assistance to promote economic growth and raise the standard of living in distressed communities in the U.S. by increasing the availability of business capital and financial services. CDFI Fund, for example, promotes access to capital and local economic growth by (1) directly investing in, supporting, and training CDFIs that provide loans, investments, financial services, and technical assistance to underserved populations and communities; (2) providing incentives to banks to invest in their communities and in other CDFIs; and (3) providing financial and other assistance to Native CDFIs and other Native entities proposing to become or create Native CDFIs through its Native Initiatives. The New Markets Tax Credit program provides investors with a tax credit for investing in communities that are economically distressed or consist of low-income populations. CDFI Fund is authorized to allocate tax credit authority under the program to Community Development Entities, which manage the program's investments in low-income community development projects. In return for a tax credit, investors supply capital to Community Development Entities.

CDFI Fund's activities have been affected by recent economic events, resulting in significant funding increases and new program initiatives in fiscal years 2009 through 2013. Funding for the competitive grant programs doubled in fiscal year 2009, with a $100 million increase provided through the Recovery Act. CDFI Fund's programs were supported in fiscal years 2012 and 2013 with funding levels of $227 million and $221 million, respectively. CMF, a program discussed above, received $80 million for fiscal year 2010 for its inaugural funding round which was awarded in the beginning of fiscal year 2011. The New Markets Tax Credit program was also expanded, with additional allocation authority provided through the Recovery Act that increased the 2008 and 2009 allocation rounds to $5 billion each. The program was supported at this same level in fiscal year 2010. In fiscal years 2011 through 2013, the program received $3.5 billion of allocation authority per year. Since the program's inception in 2000, CDFI Fund has awarded $36.5 billion of tax credit allocations to Community Development Entities.

The Small Business Jobs Act of 2010 authorized Treasury to guarantee the full amounts of notes and bonds issued by CDFIs that make investments in eligible community and economic development. Guarantees in total may not exceed $1 billion in any fiscal year and are available through September 30, 2014. As administrator, CDFI Fund was required to establish the program's regulations by September 27, 2011, 1 year after the law's enactment date, and implement the program by September 27, 2012. Additionally, the act appropriated $13.5 million to cover CDFI Fund's costs to implement and administer a bond guarantee program. CDFI Fund announced the CDFI Bond Guarantee Program in fiscal year 2011, but did not meet the mandated deadlines to establish program regulations by September 27, 2011, and stand up this program by September 27, 2012. Another key component of the CDFI Bond Guarantee Program is the financing vehicle used by CDFIs issuing bonds and notes that are 100-percent guaranteed by the federal government. Consistent with federal credit policy contained in the OMB's Circular No. A-129, the Federal Financing Bank is to purchase the CDFIs' 100 percent guaranteed issues.

The fiscal year 2014 budget proposes $225 million to fund CDFI Fund grant programs and its administration of them. Of this amount, $166 million is proposed to be used to support core programs such as the CDFI and Native American CDFI assistance programs and the Bank Enterprise Award Program. Also included in the fiscal year 2014 proposed amount is funding for the Healthy Food Financing Initiative introduced in fiscal year 2013. The Healthy Food Financing Initiative is a joint project with the Department of Agriculture and the Department of Health and Human Services that provides access to nutritious foods for those living in underserved urban and rural communities. The initiative's purpose is to eliminate food deserts in both urban and rural communities. Proposed funding for this initiative is $35 million for fiscal year 2014, a $15 million increase over the fiscal year 2013 appropriation.

The fiscal 2014 budget proposes to increase CDFI Fund's allocation authority to $5 billion for the New Markets Tax Credit program in fiscal year 2014. The budget also proposes a new allocated tax credit, the Manufacturing Communities Tax Credit, to support qualified investments in communities affected by mass layoffs and military base closures. Approximately $2 billion of credits would be provided for qualified investments approved in each year from 2014 through 2016.

International Assistance

A prosperous world economy serves the U.S. in many ways, including creating markets for U.S. goods and services and promoting stability and cooperation among nations. Treasury focuses on preventing crises and minimizing the impact of those that occur. International financial institutions, such as the International Monetary Fund and the multilateral development banks, including the World Bank, play a key role in enabling global economic growth and stability. Recent focus has been to resolve and prevent further spread of the financial crisis worldwide.

The Office of International Affairs oversees U.S. interests in international financial institutions. The U.S. participates in these institutions to support poverty reduction, private sector development, the transition to market economies, and sustainable economic growth and development; and thereby advance U.S. economic, political, and commercial interests abroad. Treasury has the responsibility for ensuring that these institutions appropriately use the resources the U.S. contributes, and for this reason reviews how these institutions use the money the U.S. government invested. Improving the effectiveness of the multilateral development banks has been a high priority for the administration. Accordingly, Treasury has been pursuing a reform agenda that emphasizes raising living standards and reducing poverty; measuring the results of U.S. contributions; and strengthening efforts to stimulate private-sector investment, promote good government and the rule of law, and fight corruption.

Exchange Stabilization Fund

The Gold Reserve Act of 1934 established the Exchange Stabilization Fund, a fund to be operated by the Secretary of the Treasury, with the approval of the President. The act authorized the Exchange Stabilization Fund to use its assets to deal in gold and foreign exchange to stabilize the exchange value of the dollar. The fund is used to implement U.S. international monetary and financial policy, including exchange market intervention policy. The fund mainly consists of three types of assets: U.S. government securities, foreign currency assets, and Special Drawing Rights.

The Exchange Stabilization Fund investment guidelines require that to ensure the highest degree of confidence in the underlying securities, the fund's investments are to be limited to claims on respective central banks, the Bank for International Settlements, and sovereign governments and their agencies.[4] The Exchange Stabilization Fund's foreign currency holdings are to be invested so as to ensure that adequate liquidity is maintained to meet anticipated intervention financing needs. Investment maturities are to be timed such that substantial funds come available on a regular basis to meet potential intervention financing needs. In addition, the investment objective of the fund's portfolio is to seek a rate of return on each of its currency components that is as high as possible over a full interest rate cycle.

Office of Technical Assistance

The Office of Technical Assistance provides technical assistance to developing and/or transitional countries to help strengthen their financial management capacities as authorized under Section 129 of the Foreign Assistance Act of 1961. The office focuses on the following five core development program areas: (1) budget and financial accountability, (2) government debt issuance and management, (3) banking and finance services, (4) revenue advisory, and (5) economic crimes. Treasury provides on-site resident advisors, as well as temporary advisors, to work with foreign government finance ministries and foreign central banks in managing public financial resources. The office's staff also monitors and evaluates projects in each developing and transitional country selected to receive assistance under one or more of Treasury's five core development areas.

Committee on Foreign Investment in the U.S.

The Committee on Foreign Investment in the U.S. was delegated the presidential function, authorized by Section 721 of the Defense Production Act of 1950, to investigate the merger or acquisition of U.S. companies by foreign persons for national security implications. The Secretary of the Treasury chairs the committee, and the Office of International Affairs manages this function on the Secretary's behalf. The committee is required to annually report on (1) whether there is credible evidence of a coordinated strategy by one or more countries or companies to acquire U.S. companies involved in research, development, or production of critical technologies for which the U.S. is a leading producer; and (2) whether there are industrial espionage activities directed or directly assisted by foreign governments against private U.S. companies aimed at obtaining commercial secrets related to critical technologies.

---

[4] The Bank for International Settlements is an international central bank whose mission is to serve central banks in their pursuit of monetary and financial stability and to foster international cooperation in those areas.

Potential Integrity Risks

We believe that integrity risks for domestic and international assistance programs include the potential (1) unauthorized release of sensitive or classified data; (2) falsification of applications or statements; (3) misuse or mismanagement of federal funds, including irregularities in the award of contracts and misallocation of grant proceeds, payments in lieu of tax credits, or federal tax credits; and (4) failure by assisted entities to deliver on promised services. Of particular concern would be contracts that may be let, or grants, or tax credits, or cash payments in lieu of tax credits that may be awarded, without following standard operating procedures that include appropriate monitoring of funded activities. In addition, we recognize program risks could exist that include the failure to promote economic growth within financially underserved areas of the U.S. or to foster economic stability in other nations. There may also be a corresponding loss of credibility with taxpayers in this country or a loss of U.S. credibility on an international level if these Treasury programs do not function as intended, or with the appropriate transparency.

In-Progress and Planned Fiscal Year 2014 Projects

Oversight of Programs Authorized by HERA (In-Progress)

The overall objective of our audit oversight of HERA programs is to assess Treasury's use of its authorities under the act. We identified distinct and separate areas of concern that we plan to review in the fiscal year 2014.

Senior Preferred Stock Purchase Agreements (In-Progress)

We plan to assess Treasury's process for providing solvency to Fannie Mae and Freddie Mac through the purchases of senior preferred stock of the entities. Specifically, we plan to assess Treasury's (1) determinations and considerations required under the act for entering into the agreements to purchases stock, (2) funding decisions, (3) monitoring the compliance with the agreements, and (4) rationale for including dividend and commitment fee requirements in the agreements. Audit work for this project began in fiscal year 2011 and is still ongoing. Given the size of Treasury's investment in Fannie Mae and Freddie Mac and Treasury's continued support of them, we plan future work in this area to evaluate Treasury's monitoring of its investment and the housing market.

Treasury's Monitoring of Government Sponsored Enterprises

We plan to evaluate Treasury's continued monitoring of its investment in the GSEs and the overall housing finance market.

Treasury's Monitoring of the Housing Finance Agency Initiative's Performance

We plan to assess Treasury's monitoring of the housing finance market indicators for assessing the health of the housing finance agencies participating in the HFA Initiative.

CDFI Fund Administration of the Capital Magnet Fund

We plan to determine if CDFI Fund established controls for awarding and administering CMF grant activities. Specifically, we plan to assess CDFI Fund's processes to (1) review whether funds were properly and timely awarded to eligible recipients and (2) ensure awardees' compliance with program requirements to include leveraging award dollars that will provide a dedicated source of funding. We also plan to assess the programs resulting from any future funding from Fannie Mae and Freddie Mac.

Oversight of Recovery Act Programs

The overall objective of our audit oversight of Treasury's Recovery Act programs is to evaluate management's accountability, control, and oversight of the Department's non-IRS funds and provide recommendations for improving operations and preventing fraud, waste, and abuse with respect to those funds. Through a series of audits, described below, we will determine if Treasury timely and effectively implemented program activities for awarding Recovery Act funding.

Payments in Lieu of Tax Credits for Specified Energy Properties (Ongoing)

We plan to determine if Treasury timely and effectively implemented activities for awarding and monitoring payments in lieu of tax credits for specified energy properties under the Recovery Act. We plan to assess the eligibility of award recipients and whether recipients are in compliance with award requirements. Audit work for this project began in April 2009 and will continue in fiscal year 2014.

We also plan to coordinate with TIGTA to determine if Treasury established and maintained internal control procedures to prevent recipients from improperly receiving both tax credits and Recovery Act payments for the same specified energy properties.

Corrective Action Verification on EcoGrove LLC Payment Under 1603 Program

We plan to determine if Treasury management took corrective action responsive to our recommendations in audit report, *Recovery Act: Audit of EcoGrove LLC Payment Under 1603 Program*, (OIG-11-103; Sept. 11, 2011).

Payments to States for Low-Income Housing Projects in Lieu of Low-Income Housing Credits (Ongoing)

We plan to determine if Treasury timely and effectively implemented activities for awarding and monitoring payments to the states in lieu of tax credits for low-income housing projects under the Recovery Act. We will assess (1) the eligibility of grant applicants at both the state and subaward level, (2) subawardees' compliance with award requirements, and (3) internal control procedures to ensure subawardees do not receive both tax credits and payments. Audit work for this project began in April 2009 and will continue in fiscal year 2014. We will coordinate with TIGTA to ensure subawardees are not receiving both Recovery Act funds and low-income housing credits for the same properties.

CDFI Fund Administration of Recovery Act Funds (Ongoing)

We plan to determine if CDFI Fund timely and effectively awarded the additional $100 million in funding provided under the Recovery Act for grant program activities. We plan to assess eligibility of potential award recipients and evaluate effectiveness of internal control over grant awards for ensuring recipient compliance with award requirements. Audit work for this project began in April 2009 and is being performed in phases. We have completed the first phase, in which we assessed the eligibility of potential award recipients. As discussed in our report, *Recovery Act: The Community Development Financial Institutions Fund Needs to Improve Its Process for Awarding Assistance to Applicants,* (OIG-11-079; July 8, 2011), we found that in awarding Recovery Act funds, CDFI Fund did not comply with certain statutory requirements of the Recovery Act We plan to complete our work on the remaining phases in fiscal year 2014.

Corrective Action Verification on CDFI Fund Recovery Act Report

We plan to determine if CDFI Fund management took corrective action responsive to our recommendations in audit report, *Recovery Act: The Community Development Financial Institutions Fund Needs to Improve Its Process for Awarding Assistance to Applicants,* (OIG-11-079; July 8, 2011).

New Markets Tax Credit Program Award Process and Compliance Monitoring (In-Progress)

We plan to assess the New Markets Tax Credit program's (1) application and tax credit allocation process, (2) assessment of the eligibility of potential award recipients, (3) internal control over and monitoring of program awards, and (4) process for ensuring recipient compliance with tax credit allocation agreements. Audit work for this project began in February 2010 with focus on the effectiveness of CDFI Fund's allocation of the increased authority provided by the Recovery Act. We completed the award phase of this project in fiscal year 2013 and plan to conclude on the compliance monitoring phase in fiscal year 2014. As part of this audit, we will follow up on issues identified in GAO's 2010 report, *New Markets Tax Credit: The Credit Helps Fund a Variety of Projects in Low-Income Communities, but Could Be Simplified,* (GAO-10-334; Jan. 29, 2010).

Treasury's Tribal Policy

The Office of Economic Policy is responsible for implementing E.O. 13175, *Consultation and Coordination with Indian Tribal Governments* (Nov. 2000), on behalf of Treasury. The E.O. requires meaningful consultation and collaboration with tribal officials in the development of federal policies having tribal implications. The order is also meant to strengthen the U.S. relationship with tribal governments and reduce the imposition of unfunded mandates on Indian tribes. In 2009, the President issued memorandum directing department and agency heads to submit to OMB a detailed plan of action for carrying out the requirements of the E.O.

We plan to assess Treasury's implementation of a tribal policy and applicable guidance for carrying out policy to consult and collaborate with tribal governments and officials when developing federal legislation, regulation, and policy having tribal implications and resolving any issues and concerns raised by tribal officials.

Other Planned Fiscal Year 2014 Projects

Bond Guarantee Program

We plan to determine if CDFI Fund implemented program activities to carry out its responsibility to administer the Bond Guarantee Program authorized by the Small Business Jobs Act of 2010.

CDFI Fund's Re-certification Process

We plan to assess the CDFI Fund' progress in re-certifying community development financial institutions for ensuring entities remain eligible to receive funding under the CDFI Fund's financial assistance and Native Initiative grant programs. This project will include evaluating the CDFI Fund's analysis of the 2006-2010 American Community Survey Census Bureau data to update eligible geographic areas for its programs based on poverty and income data

Corrective Action Verification on CDFI Fund Program Administration

We plan to assess whether CDFI Fund management took corrective action responsive to our recommendations in audit report, *Awards Made to OneUnited Bank Were Consistent with Requirements But Certain Aspects of CDFI Fund Program Administration Need to be Revisited,* (OIG-11-091; Aug. 3, 2011).

Office of Technical Assistance Programs

We plan to assess Treasury's Office of Technical Assistance administration of programs established to provide technical assistance to foreign governments and foreign central banks in developing and transitional countries. As part of this audit, we plan to evaluate the office's process for selecting central governments and banks for receiving assistance under the office's five technical assistance programs, as well as how the office selects technical experts. We also plan to assess the office's monitoring of its program projects.

Survey of the Committee on Foreign Investment in the U.S.

We plan to assess how Treasury supports the Committee on Foreign Investment in the U.S. in identifying and addressing national security concerns arising from covered transactions with foreign investors. We will also assess whether measures have been implemented to identify foreign investors who have not filed with the committee.

Transfer of Funds under the Foreign Assistance Act of 1961

The U.S. Agency for International Development transferred $66.6 million to Treasury in fiscal year 2010 for contributions to the Global Agriculture and Food Security Program Trust Fund. The agency transferred another $125 million in fiscal year 2011 funds to Treasury for contributions to the Haiti Reconstruction Fund. Under memoranda of understanding between the U.S. Agency for International Development and Treasury, we are responsible for performing periodic program and financial audits of the use of the transferred funds, and the cost of the audits may be paid from transferred funds.

We plan to assess whether Treasury administered the transferred funds in accordance with applicable laws.

Survey of the Federal Financing Bank

Created by Congress in 1973, the Federal Financing Bank is a government corporation under the general supervision of the Secretary of the Treasury. Its mission is to reduce the costs of federal and federally assisted borrowings, to coordinate those borrowings with federal fiscal policy, and to ensure that those borrowings are done in ways least disruptive to private markets. To accomplish this mission, the Federal Financing Bank has broad statutory authority to purchase obligations issued, sold, or guaranteed by federal agencies.

We plan to perform a survey of the Federal Financing Bank to identify areas that, based on our assessment of risk, should be audited in more depth.

We plan to review Treasury's efforts to assist federal agencies in closing these accounts.

Projects under Consideration for Future Fiscal Years

CDFI Fund Implementation and Administration of the Healthy Foods Financing Initiative

We plan to assess whether CDFI Fund implemented program activities for carrying out its responsibility to administer the Healthy Food Financing Initiative. Specifically, we plan to (1) determine if CDFI Fund awarded funds to eligible recipients in accordance with applicable laws and regulations, (2) ensure that CDFI Fund established and maintained proper internal control procedures and oversight over grants for ensuring that program recipients meet eligibility requirements and properly comply with award agreements, and (3) assess CDFI Fund's process for measuring the Healthy Food Financing Initiative's performance/outcomes to ensure that the program's objectives achieve its intended purposes.

Bank Enterprise Awards

We plan to assess CDFI Fund's process for awarding and monitoring awards made through the Bank Enterprise Awards Program. Specifically, we plan to (1) determine if CDFI Fund awarded the appropriated funds to eligible recipients based on qualified activities in accordance with applicable laws and regulations; (2) ensure that CDFI Fund established and maintained proper internal control procedures and oversight over the program's awards, and (3) assess CDFI Fund's process for measuring the program's performance/outcomes to ensure that the program objectives are achieved.

Single Audits

We plan to perform quality control reviews to determine if audits obtained by CDFIs were performed in accordance with the Single Audit requirements and applicable professional standards and may be relied upon for ensuring accountability of CDFI Fund awards.

CDFI Fund's Use of Single Audits

We plan to assess CDFI Fund's process for (1) reviewing Single Audit reports, (2) determining the impact any findings may have on financial assistance received from CDFI Fund, and (3) ensuring Single Audit findings are resolved.

CDFI Fund's Tracking of Awardees Across Multiple Assistance Programs

We plan to assess CDFI Fund's coordination for tracking awardees receiving awards under multiple programs to ensure funds are used appropriately in targeted markets.

CDFI Fund's Implementation and Administration of the Manufacturing Communities Tax Credit Program

We plan to assess implementation of the CDFI Fund's Manufacturing Communities Tax Credit Program. Specifically, we plan to assess the CDFI Fund's (1) process for allocating tax credits including assessments of applicant eligibility requirements, (2) internal control over program awards, and (3) monitoring recipient compliance with allocation agreements.

CDFI Program Evaluation Project

We plan to assess the CDFI Fund's progress in evaluating how and to what extent investments in CDFIs have benefitted and contributed to developing underserved communities.

Survey of Treasury's Participation in the International Monetary Fund

We plan to gain an understanding of Treasury's role for promoting U.S. policy with respect to the International Monetary Fund.

Multilateral Development Banks

We plan to gain an understanding of Treasury's process for ensuring U.S. policy is carried out through the multilateral development banks. As part of this project, we plan to assess Treasury's participation and role with respect to global initiatives.

Treasury's Global Agriculture and Food Security Program

We plan to gain an understanding of Treasury's role in the Global Agriculture and Food Security Program, including how funds are granted in accordance with applicable guidance and collectively how funds are used to improve impoverished nations.

Debt Relief Programs

We plan to gain an understanding and perform appropriate independent oversight of Treasury's role in debt reduction programs with nations indebted to the U.S. and its process for ensuring indebted nations meet eligibility requirements for relief.

Deauville Partnership Transition Fund

In the fiscal year 2014 President's budget, Treasury requested $5 million for the Deauville Partnership Transition Fund, a multi-donor trust fund administered by the World Bank, to assist members of the Deauville Partnership with Arab Countries in Transition (currently Egypt, Tunisia, Jordan, Morocco, Libya, and Yemen). As these countries go through transformations and address their diverse economic challenges, the intent of the Transition Fund is to help promote a broad reform agenda and support inclusive development. The Transition Fund provides small grants to countries for diagnostic analyses, technical advice, and initial implementation of targeted policy initiatives and reforms that demonstrate strong results. The agreed contribution from the U.S. is 20 percent of total donor contributions to the Transition Fund, or up to $50 million of an anticipated $250 million, over several years. The Deauville Partnership officially launched the Transition Fund on October 12, 2012. Several donors – including the United Kingdom, France, and Canada – immediately provided contributions.

We plan to gain an understanding and perform appropriate independent oversight of Treasury's role in the Deauville Partnership Transition Fund.

Treaties and International Agreements

We plan to determine what treaties and international agreements with foreign governments Treasury entered into on behalf of the U.S. government and Treasury's coordination and/or consultation with the Department of State in connection with those agreements.

Exchange Stabilization Fund Investment Portfolio

We plan to (1) gain an understanding of the factors considered in developing the Exchange Stabilization Fund's policy for investments in securities and foreign currency denominated assets; and (2) determine if the fund complied with policy in its purchases, management, and sales of investments and foreign currency denominated assets.

Gulf Coast Restoration Trust Fund Oversight

Issue Area Discussion

Mandate

The Gulf Coast Restoration Trust Fund was established by the RESTORE Act of Public Law 112-141. The act requires the Secretary of the Treasury to deposit in the trust fund 80 percent of all administrative and civil penalties paid by responsible parties after July 6, 2012, pursuant to a court order, negotiated settlement, or other instrument in accordance with the Federal Water Pollution Control Act in connection with the explosion on, and sinking of, the mobile offshore drilling unit Deepwater Horizon. The trust fund is to be available (1) for expenditure to help restore the Gulf Coast region from the Deepwater Horizon oil spill; (2) for undertaking projects and programs to restore and protect the natural resources, ecosystems, fisheries, marine and wildlife habitats, beaches, coastal wetlands, and economy of that region; and (3) solely to the Gulf Coast states of Alabama, Florida, Louisiana, Mississippi, and Texas to restore the ecosystems and economy of the Gulf Coast region.

Of the total amount made available for disbursement from the trust fund during any fiscal year:

- 35 percent under the Direct Component shall be available to the Gulf Coast states, in equal shares, for expenditure for ecological and economic restoration of the Gulf Coast region:

- 30 percent under the Council-Selected Restoration Component shall be disbursed to the Gulf Coast Ecosystem Restoration Council pursuant to the council's approval of its comprehensive plan to undertake projects and programs using the best available science that would restore and protect the natural resources, ecosystems, fisheries, marine and wildlife habitats, beaches, coastal wetlands, and economy of the Gulf Coast region;

- 30 percent under the Spill Impact Component shall be disbursed to the Gulf Coast Ecosystem Restoration Council for allocation to the Gulf Coast states for eligible oil spill restoration activities, pursuant to the council's approval of the state's plan to improve the ecosystems or economy of the Gulf Coast region, using a regulatory formula;

- 2.5 percent under the Gulf Coast Ecosystem Restoration Science Program Component shall be allocated to the National Oceanic and Atmospheric Administration (NOAA) for its Gulf Coast Ecosystem Restoration Science, Observation, Monitoring, and Technology Program. This program was to be established by January 2013 to carry out research, observation, and monitoring to support, to the maximum extent practicable, the long-term sustainability of the ecosystem, fish stocks, fish habitat, and the recreational, commercial, and charter fishing industry in the Gulf of Mexico; and

- 2.5 percent under the Centers of Excellence Component shall be made available to the Gulf Coast states, in equal shares, exclusively for competitive grant awards to nongovernmental entities and consortia in the Gulf Coast region, including public and private institutions of higher education, to establish centers for excellence to conduct research only on the Gulf Coast region.

Treasury's authority to administer the Gulf Coast Restoration Trust Fund terminates on the date all amounts are expended from the trust fund. The RESTORE Act provides Treasury with remedies for a state's noncompliance with the conditions of the trust fund; Treasury may cut off funding to a state until the state either repays the trust fund or the state substitutes an ineligible activity with an eligible activity.

Potential Integrity Risks

We believe that integrity risks for the Gulf Coast Restoration projects, programs, and activities include the potential (1) falsification of applications or statements; (2) failure by grantees or contractors to deliver on promised goods or services; (3) misuse or mismanagement of federal funds, including irregularities in the award of contracts and misallocation of grant proceeds, and duplication of funding for projects or programs; (4) award of grants or contracts without following laws, regulations, or standard operating procedures; (5) failure to properly monitor funded activities; and (6) funding of programs that fail to promote the restoration of the Gulf Coast region.

Audit and Investigative Activities

The act authorized Treasury OIG to conduct, supervise, and coordinate audits and investigations of projects, programs, and activities funded under the act.

In-Progress and Planned Fiscal Year 2014 Projects

NOAA's Stand-Up of the Gulf Coast Ecosystem Restoration Science Program (In Progress)

We plan to determine if the Administrator of NOAA, in consultation with the Director of the United States Fish and Wildlife Service, established the Gulf Coast Ecosystem Restoration Science Program by the RESTORE Act's mandated deadline of January 2013.

Risk Analysis of Gulf Coast State and Local Government's Internal Controls Related to Grants Management, Procurement, Financial Reporting, and Single Audit Act Reporting

We plan to assess Gulf Coast state and local government internal controls related to (1) grants management, (2) the procurement function, (3) financial reporting, and (4) Single Audit Act (A-133) reporting. This information will be used to assess overall risk of programs and activities funded by the Gulf Coast Restoration Trust Fund and as a basis for determining the nature, timing, and extent of future audit work.

Technical Review of the Council's Initial Comprehensive Plan and Related Environmental Programmatic Assessment

We plan to engage an external specialist to perform technical assessments of the initial comprehensive plan and related environmental programmatic assessment under the Council-Selected Restoration Component. We will provide contractor oversight of the technical assessments.

Technical Reviews of Gulf Coast State Plans Related to the Oil Spill Restoration Impact Component

We plan to engage an external specialist to perform technical assessments of each Gulf Coast State's plan submitted in conjunction with the Spill Impact Component. We will provide contractor oversight of the technical assessments. It should be noted that the States' environmental and economic recovery plans and the Gulf Coast Restoration Council's comprehensive plan, discussed in the preceding paragraph, are mandated by the RESTORE Act and will drive how nearly 60 percent of the trust fund's receipts will be expended on eligible activities. Accordingly, an independent assessment of the soundness of the plans is essential to the prudent use of funds.

Treasury's Establishment of a Grants Office for the Gulf Coast Restoration Trust Fund

We plan to assess Treasury's progress towards developing the necessary infrastructure for a Gulf Coast Restoration Trust Fund grants office.

Stand-Up of the Gulf Coast Ecosystem Restoration Council

We plan to assess the Gulf Coast Ecosystem Restoration Council's progress to establish an independent federal government entity, as mandated by the RESTORE Act, to oversee the restoration and economic recovery of the Gulf Coast region.

Treasury's Grants Management of the Direct Component of the Gulf Coast Restoration Trust Fund

We plan to assess Treasury administration of the Direct Component in accordance with the RESTORE Act, applicable grant laws and regulations, and Treasury policies and procedures.

Gulf Coast Ecosystem Restoration Council's Administration of the Council-Selected Restoration Component of the Gulf Coast Restoration Trust Fund

We plan to assess the Gulf Coast Ecosystem Restoration Council administration of the Council-Selected Restoration Component of the Gulf Coast Restoration Trust Fund in accordance with the RESTORE Act, applicable regulations, and Council policies and procedures.

Gulf Coast Ecosystem Restoration Council's Administration of the Spill Impact Component of the Gulf Coast Restoration Trust Fund

We plan to assess the Gulf Coast Ecosystem Restoration Council's administration of the Spill Impact Component of the Gulf Coast Restoration Trust Fund in accordance with the RESTORE Act, applicable laws and regulations, and Council policies and procedures.

Gulf Coast Ecosystem Restoration Council's Congressional Reporting Requirements as Governed by the RESTORE Act

We plan to assess whether the Gulf Coast Ecosystem Restoration Council's congressional reports meet the requirements of the RESTORE Act and regulations, and council policies and procedures, and are reliable.

Audit of Financial Statements of the Gulf Coast Ecosystem Restoration Council

A financial audit is required for the Gulf Coast Ecosystem Restoration Council pursuant to the Accountability of Tax Dollars Act of 2002. An independent public accounting firm, under contract with OIG, will audit the Council's financial statements.

Specific Audits of RESTORE Act Projects, Programs, and Activities

For selected projects, programs, and activities, we plan to assess whether (1) the RESTORE Act program's grant, contract, or cooperative agreement was awarded and is administered in accordance with the Act, applicable regulations, and policies and procedures; and (2) the program is performing in accordance with the Act, applicable regulations, and the grant, contract, or cooperative agreement.

Projects under Consideration for Future Fiscal Years

Treasury's Administration of the Centers of Excellence Component of the Gulf Coast Restoration Trust Fund

We plan to assess Treasury administration of the Centers of Excellence Component of the Gulf Coast Restoration Trust Fund in accordance with the RESTORE Act, applicable laws and regulations, and Treasury policies and procedures.

NOAA's Administration of the Gulf Coast Ecosystem Restoration Science Component of the Gulf Coast Restoration Trust Fund

We plan to assess whether NOAA developed policies and procedures to administer the Gulf Coast Ecosystem Restoration Science Component of the Gulf Coast Restoration Trust Fund in accordance with the RESTORE Act, applicable laws and regulations, and program policies and procedures.

Gulf Coast Ecosystem Restoration Council's Administrative Activities

We plan to assess whether the Gulf Coast Ecosystem Restoration Council's administrative activities are being managed in accordance with the RESTORE Act, applicable laws and regulations, and Council policies and procedures.

SBLF and SSBCI Operations

Issue Area Discussion

The Small Business Jobs Act of 2010, established two programs: SBLF and SSBCI. The Act also created within OIG the Office of SBLF Program Oversight. Under Section 4107(a) of the Act, the Special Deputy Inspector General for SBLF Program Oversight is responsible for audit and investigations related to SBLF and SSBCI programs and must report at least twice a year to the Secretary of the Treasury and the Congress on the results of oversight activities involving the SBLF program. The Special Deputy is also responsible for identifying instances of intentional or reckless misuse of SSBCI funds.

SBLF Operations

The SBLF program was created to provide capital to small banks, with incentives for those banks to increase small business lending. Generally, SBLF was open only to insured depository institutions with under $10 billion in assets as well as bank holding companies or savings and loan holding companies, each with aggregate assets of under $10 billion. Entities that met the asset-size requirement were eligible to participate in the program if they were not on FDIC's problem list or had not been removed from that list in the 90 days previous to application. SBLF also provided an option for community banks to refinance preferred stock issued to Treasury through the TARP Capital Purchase Plan or the Community Development Capital Initiative if the banks had not missed more than one dividend payment under either of these two programs. Under the SBLF program, banks may not make loans to entities with over $50 million in revenues or in original amounts over $10 million. Loans must also meet underwriting standards established by the banks' primary banking regulators.

Treasury disbursed more than $4 billion to 332 financial institutions across the country, of which 137 were institutions that used their SBLF investment to refinance securities issued under TARP. The 137 TARP banks received two-thirds of the $4 billion invested in participating banks. Institutions receiving investments under the SBLF program are expected to pay dividends to Treasury at rates that will decrease as the amount of their qualified small business lending increases. In April 2013, Treasury reported that institutions participating in SBLF had increased their small business lending by $8.9 billion over baseline levels of $36.9 billion. Moreover, Treasury reported that 90 percent of the SBLF participants had achieved small business lending increases, and 83 percent had increased their small business lending by 10 percent or more.

Potential Weaknesses Particular to SBLF

Treasury faces many challenges in ensuring that the SBLF program meets its intended objective of increasing lending to small businesses, and measuring program performance. Under the terms of the authorizing legislation, the SBLF funds are intended to stimulate lending to small businesses, but participating institutions are under no obligation to increase their small business lending activity.

Once SBLF funds were disbursed and comingled with other funds of the participating institutions, it became difficult to track how the funds were spent. Participants are also not required to report how they use Treasury's investments. Additionally, Treasury is reliant on unverified small business lending activity reported by participating institutions to measure performance and to make dividend rate adjustments. Previous audits have identified an unusually high percentage of financial institutions that inaccurately reported their quarterly small business lending gains, impacting Treasury's measurement and reporting of program accomplishments. This issue will take on greater importance as reported lending gains will be used to establish the fixed interest rates that Treasury will apply to the SBLF capital after 2 ½ years into the program. Therefore, we will continue to examine the accuracy of lending activity reported by program participants as well as assess Treasury's implementation of the fixed rate period. We will also examine the effectiveness of the program to-date and identify the factors most influencing how financial institutions have used their SBLF capital.

Finally, dividend payments, which constitute Treasury's sole source of revenue from the SBLF program, are essentially optional, as they are non-cumulative and non-accruing. Treasury has indicated that when dividend payments are missed, it will take additional measures ranging from requiring an explanation for the missed payment to electing directors to an institution's board of directors. However, these measures may be ineffective if the institution's regulator has restricted it from making dividend payments. Institutions are also under no obligation to pay off previously missed payments. We plan to evaluate the effectiveness of Treasury's efforts to identify and collect missed dividend payments.

In-Progress and Planned Fiscal Year 2014 Projects

SBLF Use of Funds 2

We plan to determine (1) how recipient institutions are using funds awarded under the SBLF program and the factors that most influenced their use of funds, (2) determine participants' plans for repayment of Treasury's investment and exit from the program, and (3) evaluate Treasury's administration of the program.

Accuracy of Dividend Rates Set for the Fixed Rate Period

We plan to determine the accuracy of small business lending activity reported by SBLF participants for the third quarter of 2013. Lending during the third quarter of 2013 will be used to determine fixed dividend rates that will be applied after the tenth quarter of SBLF funding and remain in effect for the subsequent 2 years.

Accuracy of Lending Gains Reported by Community Development Loan Funds Participating in SBLF

We plan to examine the accuracy of small business lending gains reported by Community Development Loan Funds (CDLF). Treasury relies on CDLFs to self-report small business lending gains made with SBLF funds. Because CDLFs are unregulated financial institutions, their activity reports are not subject to verification as are other regulated institutions participating in the SBLF program.

Factors Influencing the Use of SBLF Funds by Participating Institutions

We plan to determine (1) the factors that most influenced recipient uses of funds, and (2) the factors contributing to lending trends by SBLF participants with the highest and lowest small business lending activity.

Effectiveness of Treasury's Efforts to Identify and Collect Missed Dividend Payments

We plan to (1) determine the extent to which Treasury has followed its policies and procedures in levying fines and penalties on SBLF participants for late or missed dividend payments, and (2) evaluate the effectiveness of Treasury's enforcement actions.

Projects under Consideration for Future Fiscal Years

Effectiveness of the SBLF Program in Creating Jobs

We plan to determine the degree to which loans from participating institutions that met Treasury's SBLF criteria for qualified small business lending succeeded in creating jobs.

The SBLF Program Exit Process

We plan to determine if (1) participating institutions exiting SBLF were in compliance with Treasury's program requirements, (2) participating institutions received regulatory approval to exit the SBLF program, and (3) Treasury fully recouped funds invested in participating institutions that exited the program.

SSBCI Operations

SSBCI is a $1.5 billion initiative that provides participating states, territories, and eligible municipalities with funding to support state programs that provide lending to, and investment in, small businesses. SSBCI builds on new and existing models for state small business programs, including those that finance loan loss reserves and provide loan insurance, loan guaranties, venture capital funds, and collateral support. As of December 31, 2012, Treasury had awarded 57 states, territories, and municipalities $1.5 billion in SSBCI funding. States provided plans for using their funding allocations to Treasury for approval and must report quarterly and annually on results. Another key feature is that participating states receive their allocations in three increments. As of June 30, 2013, Treasury had disbursed $583 million of the funds awarded under the program. Treasury may withhold a successive increment to a state pending the results of an audit by our office.

Potential Weaknesses Particular to SSBCI

Primary oversight of the use of SSBCI funds is the responsibility of each participating state. The states are required to provide Treasury with quarterly assurances that their programs approved for SSBCI funding are in compliance with program requirements. However, Treasury will face challenges in holding states accountable for the proper use of funds as program guidance has been ambiguous in areas, and it has not set minimum requirements for state oversight activities. While Treasury issued SSBCI National Standards in May 2012 outlining a framework for states to use in designing and implementing an oversight system for SSBCI funds, implementation of the framework is optional. As a result, Treasury cannot be assured that participating states are engaging in the necessary oversight activities to ensure that program requirements are being met. Treasury will also have difficulty holding states accountable should OIG identify misuse until it provides more definitive guidance on the proper uses of SSBCI funds.

In-Progress and Planned Fiscal Year 2014 Projects

Audits of States Participating in SSBCI (Ongoing)

We have several ongoing and planned audits of selected participating states' uses of SSBCI program funds. These audits test participant compliance with program requirements and prohibitions to identify reckless or intentional misuses of SSBCI funds, which by law Treasury is required to recoup.

Effectiveness of the State Small Business Credit Initiative (Ongoing)

We plan to (1) assess the effectiveness of the State Small Business Credit Initiative in increasing access to capital for small businesses, and (2) evaluate whether Treasury's stewardship of the State Small Business Credit Initiative is adequate to ensure program effectiveness.

Availability of Funds Not Transferred Within 2 Years of Participation

We plan to (1) determine the number of participating states that have not received their full funding allocation within 2 years of participation in SSBCI, and (2) evaluate Treasury's decisions pertaining to the termination or continuance of funding for each state.

Projects under Consideration for Future Fiscal Years

Treasury's Recoupment of Misused SSBCI Funds and Handling of Compliance Issues

We plan to determine if Treasury is taking appropriate action to (1) collect funds that OIG has identified as intentionally or recklessly misused, and (2) ensure that compliance issues identified by OIG audits have been addressed.

Private Leverage Achieved by States in Receipt of their Full SSBCI Allocation

We plan to determine (1) the number of states that have received their full SSBCI allocation, (2) whether those states will meet the target private leverage ratio of 10:1, and (3) whether their other credit support programs will meet the required private leverage ratio of 1:1.

Appendix A: Office of Audit
Fiscal Year 2014 Resource Allocation

Our planned OIG staff resource utilization by the three priority areas for fiscal year 2013 is shown in the following table:

Audit Priority	Percentage of Planned Audit Resources
Audit products mandated by law	23
Work requested by Congress or externally driven	8
Self-directed work in Treasury's highest-risk areas	69
Total	**100**

Our planned OIG audit staff resource allocation by OIG Issue Area is shown in the following table:

OIG Issue Area	Percentage of Planned Audit Resources
Treasury general management and infrastructure support:	
Financial management	8
Information security	8
General management	8
Terrorist financing, money laundering, and foreign assets control	13
Government-wide financial services and debt management	7
Safety, soundness, and accessibility of financial services	19
Revenue collections and industry regulation	3
Bill and coin manufacturing, marketing, and distribution operations	3
Domestic and international assistance programs	11
Small Business Lending Fund and State Small Business Credit Initiative Operations	12
Gulf Coast Restoration Trust Fund Oversight	8
Total	**100**

Appendix A: Office of Audit Fiscal Year 2013 Resource Allocation

The table below shows planned OIG audit staff allocation by Treasury headquarters operational component and bureau:

Treasury Component	Percentage of Planned Audit Resources
Departmental Offices:	
Domestic Finance	9
Office of the Assistant Secretary for Management and Chief Financial Officer	8
Small Business Lending Fund	6
State Small Business Credit Initiative	7
Community Development Financial Institutions Fund	5
Office of the Chief Information Officer	4
Gulf Coast Restoration Trust Fund	8
Other Departmental Offices	4
Bureaus:	
Office of the Comptroller of the Currency	18
Bureau of the Fiscal Service	14
Financial Crimes Enforcement Network	10
Mint	2
Bureau of Engraving and Printing	2
Alcohol and Tobacco Tax and Trade Bureau	3
Total	**100**

Appendix B: Index of In-Progress and Planned Fiscal Year 2014 Audits by Issue Area

Appendix C: Index of In-Progress and Planned Fiscal Year 2014 Audits by Bureau/Office

Multi Bureau

Departmental Offices

Bureau of Engraving and Printing

Bureau of the Fiscal Service

Alcohol and Tobacco Tax and Trade Bureau

Appendix D: Index of Projects under Consideration for Future Fiscal Years

Appendix D: Index of Projects Under Consideration for Future Fiscal Years

Appendix D: Index of Projects Under Consideration for Future Fiscal Years

Appendix D: Index of Projects Under Consideration for Future Fiscal Years

Abbreviations

AWG	administrative wage garnishment
BEN	Bureau of Engraving and Printing Enterprise Network System
BEP	Bureau of Engraving and Printing
BFS	Bureau of the Fiscal Service
BPD	Bureau of the Public Debt
BSA	Bank Secrecy Act
CDFI	Community Development Financial Institutions
CHIPRA	Children's Health Insurance Program Reauthorization Act of 2009
CMF	Capital Magnet Fund
Dodd-Frank	Dodd-Frank Wall Street Reform and Consumer Protection Act
E.O.	Executive Order
FDIC	Federal Deposit Insurance Corporation
FinCEN	Financial Crimes Enforcement Network
FISMA	Federal Information Security Management Act
FMS	Financial Management Service
FRB	Federal Reserve Bank
GAO	Government Accountability Office
HERA	Housing and Economic Recovery Act of 2008
HFA	Housing Finance Agencies
IPERA	Improper Payments Elimination and Recovery Act of 2010
IPERIA	Improper Payments Elimination and Recovery Improvement Act of 2012
IRS	Internal Revenue Service
IT	information technology
JAMES	Joint Audit Management Enterprise System
MSB	money services businesses
OCC	Office of the Comptroller of the Currency
OFAC	Office of Foreign Assets Control
OIG	Office of Inspector General
OMB	Office of Management and Budget
OTS	Office of Thrift Supervision
Plan	Joint Implementation Plan
Recovery Act	American Recovery and Reinvestment Act
RESTORE Act	Revived Economics of the Gulf Coast States Act of 2012
SBLF	Small Business Lending Fund
SSBCI	State Small Business Credit Initiative
TARP	Troubled Asset Relief Program
TIC	Treasury International Capital
TIGTA	Treasury Inspector General for Tax Administration

Abbreviations

TNet	Treasury Network
Treasury	Department of the Treasury
TTB	Alcohol and Tobacco Tax and Trade Bureau
XBRL	eXtensible Business Reporting Language

www.ingramcontent.com/pod-product-compliance
Lightning Source LLC
Chambersburg PA
CBHW080301180526

45167CB00006B/2615